From Monster
to Butterfly

By *John Fisher*

Dorrance Publishing Co
585 Alpha Drive
Pittsburgh, PA 15238
Visit our website at www.dorrancebookstore.com

ISBN: 979-8-8860-4414-0
eISBN: 979-8-8868-3835-0

Contents

"Please Hear Me!!" (a victim's cry for help)........................v

From Monster to Butterfly..vii

Introduction..xi

Facts..xi

You Can Change Too..............................xiv

The Journey Begins..................... xvi

Part I: The Evolution of a Monster............................*1*

Stage I: Pre-Assault....................... 3

Stage II: Set Up: Grooming to Assaults...............31

Stage III: Aftermath/False Remorse.......41

Trying To Find Normalcy.................... 43

Second Girlfriend................................46

Third Girlfriend................................48

Stage IV: Forgiveness..................... 63

   A. Beginning...Self............63

   B. Love Your Enemies......73

Part II: The Butterfly:....................79

Stage V. You Are a Survivor......................... 81

You Are a Butterfly................................86

Scars Into Stars...............................87

In Closing....................................88

Food For Thought.............................93

One Very Last Thing.........................94

Please Hear Me!!

HOPE. This book was written to give HOPE to all of the victims of the world whose lives have been devastated by mental, physical, psychological, and or sexual abuse.

"I am here to tell you today that there is HOPE for us all!"

I dedicate this book to all victims. I have been through some of your pain, and I wish to share with you the HOPE that I have been blessed with through the years. (Twenty-five percent of all royalties, over and above expenses, will be donated to different Victim Advocacy Organizations (Throughout the US.)

May your "Higher Power" continue to or begin to bless your life with peace and love.

We do not have to go through this life in hell and torment, give HOPE and LOVE a chance—again.

I would love to share this book with all victims of the world; Lord knows there are way too many.

>>>To all the programs that are out there helping victims in their recovery process, I reach out to you as well. Here is a book that was written by a victim and now a survivor, to give hope to victims. To give hope to them that now is the time for them to take their control back and to live in peace, freedom, and to empower them once again. Victims need to know that they are innocent; they must know that they did not cause any of what happened to them. God has wept for them and so loves them… Their pain can ease, with a lot of hard work and determination. Destroying people's lives is not normal. How many times have you asked yourself, "Why was all of these things happening to me? Why?" By reading this book you will see how some of the many different pieces of our lives make up who we are as a person (good and bad things). We all still have total control of whom we choose to become. No matter what has happened to us, we still have the power and control over our thoughts, feelings, and behavior. We can't change our past; we are architects of our destiny.

In this book *From Monster to Butterfly*, I will not only be sharing with you facts, but first hand things that I have lived through, I personally have thought, felt, myself.

I will share with you personally that a person just doesn't wake up one day and decide to devastate the lives of many people; there is a combination of things that happen to them. Soon, they make the choices to act out the way that they do.

If you have always wondered why a person chooses to hurt others like this, here maybe a little light to shine upon this very question.

Again, I wrote this book to give HOPE to many people, to some of the many victims that are still suffering with their abuses today and don't know how to cope any longer. There is and has always been HOPE. I would like to help you see this path as I did—through time. It is by the very Grace of God that I'm sharing this book with all who are in dire need of Hope, Peace, Serenity, and Empowerment back in their lives.

Introduction

We will be taking a look at one of society's most horrendous human behaviors—pedophilia. We hear of these crimes almost every day, along with the devastating effects it has on the victims their entire lives. Good news is with hard work and determination, the victim can take back control over their lives once again and live a more peaceful life.

Facts

Pedophilia has to be one of the most disgusting, <u>one</u> of the most devastating crimes against children. Pedophilia is nothing new; this behavioral disorder has infected too many children for centuries, yes, from the very beginning of time. Pedophilia has been called many different things, justified by many different cultures, societies, even religions over the centuries. When modern society began to see the devastating affects all of this has on the child's entire life and their families, slowly things began to change. Since no one knew much about it, this monster was still feared and shoved into the closets of world's cultures for centuries, yes, millennia. The old adage "out of sight, out of mind" theory I guess. "Just ignore it and it will soon go away" has never worked; things just got worse, if that was even possible.

Pedophilia, there is no cure, no medication, no operation, and no "magic wand" that will cure this behavioral disorder. Some professionals call pedophilia a mental illness. Others declare it a behavioral disorder, a habit like smoking, drug addiction, alcoholism, gambling, etc.

The good news is that pedophilia can be managed, controlled, and monitored if the person truly chooses to do so. It takes a lot of very hard work, plus allot of self-discipline. This choice and sex offender therapy will help the pedophile to maintain some stability within their life. The pedophile is not cured; they can manage this problem and live a good life as long as they choose to stay away from children and other high-risk behaviors (for that person). Pedophiles can be male or female; a pedophile of either gender is a destructive force against the children that they prey on. Some believe to this very day that a boy that is sodomized by an older female will have fewer problems than if a male raped them; this is totally bogus, false, untrue, a lie. Having a person to grow up sensing that their self-worth as a human being is tied into their "appearance and/or sexual performance" is so devastating to that person.

Since this is a male child that was raped by his babysitter, sister, neighbor, cousin, etc., then if he grows up very sexually active—

"Oh, this is just how males are."

This adult/VICTIM is still growing (I meant growing) through hell on the inside of them as much if they were raped by anyone else.

One could argue all day, "Well, this is just how YOU chose to act out by this. How about most all the other children that have been molested by older females and are leading normal lives right now." I will leave you with this thought on this matter: "That is the mentality that society has had for thousands of years, yes, I meant thousands of years; this has evolved into one of the cultural dysfunctions of today." I remember so clearly my dad saying to me, "I should have taken you to one of those 'Houses' in the city and have one of those women work you over a few times in bed." (Trust me when I say that I cleaned up what my dad really said to me that day.) My dad was serious; he was also hurting and felt helpless in helping me work through my issues that I so clearly had at that time.

At that time, no one knew much about pedophilia, even cared to really, nor really had any idea on how to confront it.

People that went into a mental health facility were placed on the AA (Alcoholic Anonymous) wing. The professionals, at the time, really did not know how to place nor treat pedophilia. Still, pedophilia has infested children almost since the very beginning of time. Thank God, the treatment for pedophilia has really evolved and can help all those that truly want to change, through their hard work, determination, and perseverance. Out of all the hell that any one family may go through, having one of your children molested has to be one of the most devastating things that could ever happen.

Pedophilia knows no barriers as far as female or male victims, race, creed, or color. They're male, and female predators, Catholic, Protestant, Methodist, or Jew etc. There are pedophiles in every facet of society and culture (some cultures seem to tolerate more than other cultures) at any socioeconomic levels, rich, poor, sick, or healthy.

There are no boundaries that have not and will not be crossed; there is nothing that is neither "taboo" nor sacred to the pedophile.

These molestations will remain with the victims to one degree or another to their last days. Some victims are so troubled, so debilitated in toxic shame and toxic guilt, some may choose to shorten their "days" through suicide, which is so sad. Pedophiles devastate the child victim, the children are engulfed in this hell and torment for life, but this hell and torment touches their entire family as well. The parent's peace of mind; no one can imagine how devastated a parent can be when they find out that their child has been molested. The helplessness. powerlessness, the anger, and rage must be unbearable. They are the very one(s) that are supposed to protect their child(ren) and to not sense that something maybe going on and they didn't do anything to stop it is almost as bad as losing a child to death. The parent(s) feel so debilitated in toxic shame, toxic guilt, anger, and rage, not only at the predator but themselves as well. The shockwaves ripple through the whole family for generations as well. *Then to add to this unbearable pain is the insult that most all molestation of children is by someone that the family and the child knows, trusts, and even loves in some cases.* Even more soul shattering is when the predator is a parent or close family member.

I'm not saying any of this to scare a parent. I am sharing these things to encourage the parent(s) to be aware of their child's friends, who their children hang out with, who is hanging out with them. (Including family, friends, and neighbors). Be aware of any major behavioral pattern changes in your children; just stay aware. Please ask when you see your child around questionable people, places, or things for their safety, no matter how upset the child may become or how unapproachable that person that they are with may be. This is your child; <u>DO</u> all you can to protect them. Above all else—listen to when your child says something bad is happening to them; 99.9 percent of the time something is happening. Stay as calm as one can be during this time. Get as many details as you can from the child. Please trust the child and notify the authorities, promptly; let the authorities do all of the investigating. Help the authorities all one can. The main focus for the parent(s) needs to be to reassure and help your child through all of this the best you can.

The child and the parent(s) both will need some kind of therapy to help them navigate through this hellish ordeal they have went through.

I understand in a culture where there is no way for many single parent families, or in most cases where both parents must have full time jobs, it is very difficult to give your children the attention that they so need/deserve. I say this next out of the deepest respect for you/your family:

Do your best to spend quality time (I don't mean quantity) with your family as often as one can—for if you do not, someone else could...

Above all else, have your child(ren) know that they can talk to you about anything that is troubling them—at any time. Be vigilant, stay aware of your child's friends. Please stay aware of any behavioral changes. This is your child; <u>DO</u> all you can to protect them. Make sure they know that ***YOU*** Love Them; if you don't, someone else will.

Another word of caution: Not every pedophile/sex offender is on a state/federal registry! This is very sad, but very true; we all hear about this in the news way too often.

You Can Change Too

This information can be very valuable in the treatment of victims and predators. I have been a victim and a survivor. I'm sharing some of my journey to becoming a survivor with you today. There are not very many books out there today to address these issues that are covered here. I have been a victim of mental, physical, psychological, and sexual abuse as a child.

As one reads through my story, they may think, "What was his problem? I went through ten times worse, and my life has turned out pretty good." One will see that many things in our lives will affect different people in different ways, which can encourage *their* choices and their behaviors throughout their lives.

I begin to share some of the hell that I went through, as a child (knowing that others have gone through much worse) growing up. So some may see some of what I went through as a child victim, and now I'm sharing some of my story with others. (Which can be a form of future healing.)

"Forgiveness Process": learning to forgive all the people that have hurt me; also learning to forgive myself as well. (A work that still is in process to this day.) If I don't love myself, how can I ever love anyone else?

Which helped to motivate me into my "Survival Process," where I am today.

Learning to understand a part of you that you want to hate, to get rid of, and to erase from your memory is not easy. It is truly a battle, a daily battle. Now I have *chosen* to be a Survivor and wanting to share my story with you. To show you that there is HOPE, and where there is HOPE, LOVE will soon follow, with change close to follow.

Wise men have said: "There is Good and evil in <u>all</u> of us (there is that monster and that butterfly in us <u>all</u>.) The only difference being is the one that <u>we</u> choose to feed at any given moment. WE make the choice to be good or evil; no one else determines our future like we do ourselves."

"Is 'Free Will' all that great of a blessing?" Yes, it is!! "Which one do you choose to feed in your life—the Monster or the Butterfly?"

Please note, I am not a counselor. I have no initials before or after my name (MSW, PhD, Dr., etc.). Other than the "School of Hard Knocks" is what I have to share with you.

To ALL Victims: If you have wondered "WHY?" these things happened to you, maybe this book could shed a little light onto some of those questions that you have been wondering about for so long.

PLEASE, this is by no means trying to justify any/all of the things that happened to you; there is NO justifiable reason WHY, no way—ever.

To ALL Predators that are still devastating the lives of their victims, or you may still feel nor want to see all the devastation and the hell that you are still causing the victim AND their entire family, with your horrific behavior. How you may still feel that what you are doing is not all that bad—here is your "WAKE UP CALL!"; here is your sign to "STOP!" putting these precious people through the hell that you yourself have gone through or are still going through. There is HOPE—Seek and Find It TODAY!

I will soon walk you through five stages that I went through in becoming a survivor. Now all of these stages will take time. By reading this book you will not be magically healed. I hope that you will be able to come to a better understanding of the things that have happened to you, around you, and some of the choices that were made either by you or to you. To all victims: I know this may be hard to understand right now, but you were and are innocent of the hell you are going through; choose to become a survivor!

The Journey Begins

As I have said before, NO one just wakes up and begins to harm someone... There is a process, a change, choices that we all choose to make to advance to the next steps in an "Offending Cycle." Here I have explained five stages one may go through. Anyone could go through many more stages or less stages. What is important to know of in the stages is that there is a progression, and when we soon know this, we can stop ourselves, refocus our thoughts, our behavior, so we do not harm anyone or ourselves. Here is an example of Five Stages that one may go through.

Stage I: Pre-Assault: During this stage I will be sharing the early parts of my life as a child. Stage II: Set Up: Grooming and Assault Stage: Here I will explain more of the distorted choices, justifications, and how one tries to rationalize, to oneself, what one was doing in order to continue their behavior. I will be sharing some of the set-up and grooming that a predator may do.

Stage III: Aftermath/False Remorse: Here is where a predator may try to apologize, to the victim, for the things that the predator has done to them.

Stage IV: Forgiveness: I was filled with hate, anger, rage, and revenge. I hated my mother, father, and almost everyone in my life. I was filled with hurt, pain, and my scars and wounds ran deep into my soul. I also hated myself. I was damaged goods, and I felt like I was also hated by all because of the things that happened to me. One of my biggest steps on the road to my Survival process was "Forgiveness." This became one of the biggest turning points in my life; one will see how hard this process is but how important it really is for all of us.

Step V: You Are A Survivor: We should not take this journey alone; we really need all the help we can get. Becoming a survivor is so important to us, our mental health, to our souls, and to our very spirits. This step could take the longest, and may even take years. I felt so all alone; I felt that I didn't have anyone that really cared for me. It was by going through the forgiveness process that I saw that I had all kinds of people that loved me and cared for me.

I thought because of all the hell that I went through, that God hated me, and He didn't want anything to do with me. I had problems with God. If He loved me, why did He not help me when I cried out to Him for help? Where was He when I needed Him! I was blaming God as WELL for all that I was going through. If God will not help me, or love me, no one does. Does any of this sound familiar to any of you? Also, read other books to help you understand as well. There now are programs that are developed to help you no matter where you are in this process. Remember, you don't have to live in your pain any longer; there is help for the victims and for the predators now. Please seek this help ASAP. Here is my story, and I truly hope that it will help you. I hope that it will answer some of the questions that have weighed so heavily on your heart of "WHY?" "WHY me!?" God so LOVES you; it's your turn to learn to LOVE yourself—so you will soon love others.

Part I: The Evolution to a Monster

Stage I
Pre-Assault

Social psychology is the scientific study of how people's thoughts, feelings, and behaviors are influenced by the actual, imagined, or implied presence of others.

Social Psychology plays a major role in everyone's life, how we all choose to interpret it, accept it, manage it, and how we choose to react to these issues in our lives could define our entire beings, who we are, even who we could be at any one time—as adults. Some of us may have grown up in hell; hell may have been all around us, even engulfed and tried to consume us; all of this doesn't have to define who we are today any longer. Here I will share a little of my childhood with you.

In the Beginning

Grandma was a very strict, devoted Christian lady (Dad's mom). I really did not know much about my grandfather, other than he was part Cherokee Indian. My dad had one sister and one brother. They grew up during the Great Depression, and his family went through some very tough times as well—as most all people of that day. I'm guessing that my dad did not see much love or attention from his dad, because I felt that I didn't seem to receive much from him.

My dad, as an adult, the world was in the middle of WWII, and my dad and uncle signed up for the navy. They both had seen more bloodshed and death than any human being should ever have to. Dad had finished two to three tours in the navy before the war had ended. My dad, like most of the veterans, was very tired, weary, and needed rest.

My dad very seldom talked about the war. I'm guessing that it was so horrific he just didn't want to talk about it, maybe only with his very close compatriots—if even then.

Mother grew up in a very male dominated German/Irish family. Mom grew up with a brother and one sister. Her dad was German, her mom was Irish, and she also went through WWII and some very hard times as well. Her dad served in WWI and was shot and lost one of his lungs. He drank and smoked a lot, and from some stories I have heard Mom tell, he was a very strict disciplinarian. (Just like she turned out to be.) My uncle did something wrong one day, as a child, and my grandfather chained him to a tree outside for a long time as his punishment.

Things like this would be unheard of today, right? Mom grew up and married a nice gentleman, and Mom and he seemed to be getting along very well. There seemed to be one problem, though: Mom wanted a family, and he could not give her one. Mom was in a very tough situation; she had married into a devoted Catholic family, and Catholics paid very close attention to Church Doctrine. (When someone was married, this was a lifetime commitment, and divorce was not an acceptable option.) How Mom was able to divorce this gentleman, I cannot remember. She did, and soon, she met Dad. I can still remember the times that Mom had some good things to say about Dad. How when she first met him, she fell "head over heels" in love with him. How handsome he was, how she soon wanted to spend the rest of her life with him. It was not long after that they got married.

My dad and my grandfather (Mom's dad) got along very well from what I understand from the stories from Mom and Grandma. They both were in wars of their days, they both loved to drink, Grandpa smoked his cigarettes, Dad with his cigars, and they loved to play cards at one of the bars that they went to frequently. So, these were a couple of "Good Ole' Boys" that got along pretty well.

Mom began to see, all too quickly, that Dad's drinking was going to be a problem in this family. I never really knew what all happened during the war, but things must have really torn Dad up more than any of us ever knew. Dad had problems keeping a job for any length of time. He would work for a while, then get on a drinking spell, lose a job. Go deeper into a drinking spell. All hell would soon break at home. Mom soon would leave Dad and go back home. After, Dad would come to his senses, ever so briefly; he would go to Mom and beg her to come back to him. Mom soon went back to Dad, and this cycle went on for many years. These were true signs of alcoholism, which Dad always denied. At one point in Mom and Dad's life, things seemed to be going pretty good. Dad was going to work, coming home at a decent time; things were good. Dad soon talked Mom into moving back with him, and she did. Dad was working pretty well, supporting them okay, and they soon decided to begin a family.

Mom said that she was so excited, so happy. She just hoped that Dad would soon settle down and help raise this family. Dad promised Mom that he would always be there for her; Mom wanted to believe him. It was a very joyful time when Mom found out that she was pregnant. Mom and Dad were both overjoyed, ecstatic, and their love grew. Dad swore that he would be there for Mom and the baby; he wanted to settle down and be a responsible father. I'm sure that Dad met everything that he said to Mom that day. Mom wanted to believe him so badly that she did believe him, once again. Dad was true to Mom and kept his word, and he was by her side all of the way. Soon, Mom began to have complications with her pregnancy. I cannot remember exactly what it was. The day she had a miscarriage, she thought her dreams of having a family were over. Mom thought this was strictly her fault, and Dad thought that it was his fault. Their doctor said it is just one of those horrible things that happens sometimes. Doc reassured Mom that her and Dad were perfectly healthy and that they could always try again. Needless to say, Mom and Dad both were devastated. Dad soon went back to drinking instead of staying with Mom. Mom was racked with debilitating guilt; she didn't want anything to do with Dad; they went their separate ways again, for…a while.

The initial response to losing a child has to be devastating, overwhelming, and the pain has to be unbearable. Along with all the mental gymnastics, toxic guilt, and toxic shame that both Mom and Dad must have gone through would be horrendous.

So these were very dark times for both Mom and Dad. Mom chose to go back to her mom, while Dad chose his old friend, alcohol, and they lost themselves for a while. After they worked through their grief in their own ways, Mom still wanted a family, and Dad wanted to get back with Mom. Mom has said so many times that Dad was a caring and loving person if he would leave that alcohol alone. She loved him still after all that they went through. Dad has always had a problem sharing his thoughts and feelings with anyone, really. Dad had a very troubled soul; there was so much going on inside of Dad that he thought that the only way to some type of sanity was through drinking. He kept all of this bottled up and pushed down deep inside of him and he never shared whatever it was bothering him with anyone; that's the way men handled things back then, by themselves—mostly. Once again Dad moved in with Mom for a while. Mom wanted to see how Dad was before moving out again. Things were soon going well, and it was just a matter of time that they moved into a place of their own once again.

It was a short time after this Mom was pregnant once again, and she was cautiously elated, as was Dad. It's like they wanted to let the whole world know that Mom was with child, but at the same time no one really knew for sure yet.

Mom kept all of her doctor's appointments, listened to all of the doctor's suggestions. The further along that Mom was, the more confident both Mom and Dad were about having their first child. Mom had a few small complications along the way, but her doctor was confident that things would progress along normally to full term. Mom was getting a little scared and concerned the closer it came to having this baby; she wanted this child so badly. Her mom and dad were doing all they could to help Mom. Grandma prayed that this baby would be born healthy, with no problems. Not only for the baby's sake, but for Mom's mental health as well. Mom did go through some very deep depression from her miscarriage, and they didn't know how Mom would be if she would lose this child too. So, prayers were high from all that knew the family. Mom and Dad have planned for this child for some time. They were thinking about different names to call the child, how they planned to raise the child.

Back then they didn't know the sex of the child until after they heard their first cries; of course, Dad wanted a son, Mom was just wanting a healthy child. Soon, their wait was over; they had a fine, healthy baby boy, with a great set of lungs. When the doctor swatted me on the bottom to make sure I was breathing, the doctor then got a surprise and got his face washed. The doctor found out that I had good kidneys as well. Yes, this was me. I was blessed into this world, yelling, screaming, with all fingers and toes and two very happy parents.

I can still remember some of the stories that Mom told me about how, at first, the nurses couldn't tell if I was a girl or boy; I was dressed in pink?

On a few occasions Mom almost lost me due to one sickness or another. How she became so overprotective of me to the point of smothering my very childhood out of me through her loving care and concern to keep me safe and alive. (As that child, growing up, I didn't see it or feel it that way at the time.)

It was a short time that Dad was soon back to his old ways, losing his job, not being able to support now the family, right back to drinking once again, and this caused even more problems. Mom needed help with me, and she was getting little help from Dad at all.

Dad came home late in the evening, drunk, with a cold supper sitting on the table waiting for him. Mom and Dad had so many verbal fights; it really scared me (as I grew a little older).

We were like a yo-yo, leaving Dad, going back home to Grandma. Dad would seem to be back on the wagon for a while. Soon, Mom and I would move back with him, a revolving door family it seemed, which is not good for any family.

My first real memories began when I was about four years old, good memories at that time. It was wintertime, and Dad and I were outside playing in the snow. He was showing me how to build a snowman, how to make snowballs, all of that great, fun kid stuff, right? I was getting cold, my clothes were wet from the snow. Dad and I was having a lot of fun. Then Mom walked out on the back porch and told Dad to get me inside before I catch pneumonia. I let out a big sigh of disapproval, as Dad said: "Okay, we'll be inside in a few minutes, hon."

"If he gets sick you will be taking care of him; you will worry about him, not me," Mom replied angrily, as she walked into the house and slammed the back door.

Dad looked at me, shook his head. "I guess we better go in or we will never hear the last of it," Dad said with a smile. He picked me up, tossed me over his shoulder, and we went in for the day. I was giggling and laughing all the way into the house.

A lot of my early childhood was kind of cloudy. I don't know if this was on purpose, a choice that I made, or if I just wanted to block things out because of the traumatic effects that things had on me at the time. I do remember many of the verbal fights that Mom and Dad had, most all of them was when Dad began drinking heavy again.

Mom would complain a lot to Dad about not having a job; of course, there was a family to care for now. We may not have money for bread or milk, but Dad would be out and about late in the evening and come home drunk. Where did he get the money for the alcohol? Dad told Mom that he may pay for one or two drinks, and his buddies would buy the rest. Mom asked on a few occasions, "Do they force these drinks down you? Is your bottom glued to that bar stool; you can get up and leave, right?" Then the arguments began. This was one of the times that we were living at Grandma's house. I was about five years old. Dad came home late, drunk, and Mom was on him the second that he walked in the door.

"I called you right before supper. Did you get my message?" asked Mom.

"Yes," Dad said as he walked toward the kitchen.

"Two hours later you decide to come home?" Mom said angrily.

"I'm home, woman, what else do you want?" Dad said loudly to Mom.

"I want us to be a family. I want you to be a part of—" Mom began to say. I was sitting on the couch when the verbal arguments began, and I was scared to death. Mom and Dad were screaming at each other in the middle of the front room. I began to cry; I began to kick my little legs, crying and begging for them to stop. I didn't want Dad to hurt Mom, and I didn't like to see Dad like this at all. The more I cried, the more that I kicked my legs; they soon stopped, and Mom would focus on me, and Dad would soon stomp off to the kitchen to eat his cold supper. (No microwaves at this time.)

It would be a day or two later, things would be calm again until Dad acted out again.

All I know was that I loved my dad, and I didn't like it at all when Mom and him were fighting like this. I love my mom; she was my rock; she was there for me all of the time. Dad was there part time. I surely didn't want anything to happen to Mom.

Now I know that all of this was not Dad's fault. Mom and Grandma didn't make things easy at all. Mom and Grandma had their personal issues, and so did Dad. Both of the women went through hell in their lives; so did Dad. The major problems were they either didn't know how to talk about these things or didn't want to talk about them. All I know is that most of their thoughts and feelings were stuffed deep inside of them, and this volcano was ready to explode. At times Dad felt that he could not do anything right: Dad got a job, he was in construction, he was in the heat all day long, he got off from work, stopped by the tavern to have a couple of brews before going home to supper. When Dad got home, he heard Mom complain about something almost every day. Hearing all of this—most of the time—would push anyone away and not want to come right home after work.

When Dad didn't have a job, he wasn't going to stay at home and hear all of the complaining, so he would spend even more time away from home—at the tavern, and Mom complained about that. This wore even more on the fragile relationship with Mom and Dad, and Dad would fall into his depression. He was raised in an old-fashioned family, where the male took care of his family. It was the male that was in full charge of the family. The man was the one with a job: it was the male that paid the bills; it was the male that protected and cared for all of his family's basic needs.

How bad he must have felt knowing that he is not doing that, plus trying to fight what other demons he chose to have at the time. Then to have your wife harping, complaining, and degrading you almost at your every turn was not helping things at all. Dad must have been feeling like a failure, having Mom reminding him of all the things that he wasn't doing did not help him at all. When Dad was feeling his worst, he would begin to drink hard liquor, and he was very mean when he came home drunk. Like this night that is so vivid to me as if it happened just yesterday. (It happened over sixty-plus years ago, at the time of this writing.)

This was another one of those nights that Dad came home, and he was very drunk. In seconds, he and Mom were screaming and hollering at each other. They were nose to nose at this point. I was extremely scared; this was the worst that I have ever seen them. I began to cry out load, just kicking my legs and screaming at one point for them to stop.

"PLEASE STOP!" I cried out. I was begging for them to stop their arguing.

Dad walked over to me and yelled in my face, "Shut the h— up or I'll give you something to cry about!"

I was just rattled with fear at this point. I cried even more, and I was shaking in fear. Dad grabbed my arm and pulled me up and off the couch; he was yelling and screaming at me all the way into the bedroom. I know that my little feet did not hit the floor more than once all the way into the room. Then Dad tossed me into my bed. I slammed up against the wall; my breath was knocked out of me briefly. I began to plead with my dad: "Stop, Daddy, stop. I'm sorry," I cried out to him, still trembling to the point that I almost wet all over myself.

"Shut the h— up, you little Mama's Boy, or I'll beat you and give you something to cry about," Dad continued to yell at me as he came over to my bed.

"Leave him alone and get in here. I need to talk to you!" Mom yelled at Dad.

"Woman, I'm going to teach this little baby a lesson once and for all," Dad said as he began to reach for his belt.

"I'm calling the police, I have had enough," Mom yells, as she goes over to the phone.

"I'll take care of you later!" Dad said as he stomped off to the front room and told Mom to get off the phone. "Your little baby is okay, I didn't hurt him," Dad said.

I was so scared, I was trembling from head to toe, and I really thought that Dad was going to kill me.

I have never seen him this enraged before. I covered myself up in my blankets. I covered my head with my pillow and cried myself to sleep, not knowing if I would wake up the next day or not.

Looking back to that time, I saw hurt, pain, anger, and rage in Dad's eyes. This raging volcano erupted, releasing some of that pent-up rage that was brewing on the inside of him. When I woke up the next morning, Dad was not there. I felt a little bit of relief. Mom asked, "How are you doing, son?" as she was checking out the deep-purple bruising on my arm. I started crying again as I was trying to tell Mom how scared I was.

I then said: "Mom, I'm sorry if I made Daddy mad. I'm sorry if I got you in trouble," I cried out through my tears.

Mom hugged me tightly and told me: "Son, you didn't do anything wrong; it was your drunken', good-for-nothing father. It was all his fault. You had nothing to do with all of that," Mom tried to reassure me. Still, I felt that if I was a good little boy and if I didn't say or do anything, that all of that would not have happened.

"Where is Daddy now, Mom?" I asked.

"I don't believe this, after all he put you through last night and you are asking where your dad is at?"

"Is he coming back home soon?" I asked.

"We (Mom and Grandma) told him to leave for a couple of days and calm down, and if he ever acts like that again I'm going to have him thrown in jail," Mom explained. All I know is that I wanted my dad; I didn't want the dad I had last night. I love my dad, but not the dad like he was the night before. I still was scared of my dad after that; when I heard his voice, I was very nervous until I knew what mood he was in.

I was about six years old when my first sister was born, Sharon. I wanted a brother, of course, but I got a sister instead. I had mixed thoughts about having a sister. I was happy to have someone I could play with and to have fun with; it was pretty hard being the only kid in the family. There was little to do; the adults didn't always want to play, so I kind of felt alone at times, but now I had a sister.

Then, I had been the only child for so long. I kind of liked the attention. I might not get as much now. The sister thing was pretty cool at first, then I saw that she was getting most of the attention, and no one was tending to my needs; this was not cool at all. A lot of things happened when I was six. Just before I received my sister, my grandpa died (Mom's dad), one of Dad's closest friends. I lost my friend, my grandfather, to death; I lost my dad again to his drinking, yet again. Then this was my first year of school, and this just didn't go over well with me at all.

I was hardly ever around other children very much. I had other cousins, whom I hardly ever saw at that time. Mom and Dad hardly had any friends come over to visit that would have children, and now I was in a room with all of these kids and an older woman, and I had no idea whom she was nor did I care. I wanted to leave, I wanted to get out of there and go back home. Even though Mom and Grandma tried to get me ready for this day, talking to me about school, how much fun I will have there. All the other children I will be meeting and will be able to play with, how cool all of this will be—I wanted nothing to do with any of it.

Mom was trying to leave, and I was holding fast to the hem of her dress. The teacher came over and began to talk nicely to me, asking me all kinds of things. "Do you like to color?" she asked. I nodded my head yes. "We have all kinds of nice coloring books for you to choose from; we all like to color a lot. Come, let me show you the different books we have for you," the teacher said as she held out her hand to me. I pulled back behind Mom for protection; I didn't know what this woman was going to do to me.

"Go with the teacher. She wants to show you the different coloring books that you can color in today."

"If you color a nice picture, maybe you can take it home to your mom to put up on the ice box," the teacher said.

I looked up to Mom, and Mom nodded her head yes. I slowly loosened my grip on Mom's dress and reluctantly went with the teacher over to the coloring table, where some of the kids were already having fun. The next thing I knew, the time flew by, and Dad was there to pick me up from school. On the way home, I was going on and on how great of a day that I had, all of the different things that I did and the cool kids that I met; the first day of school was awesome.

The very next year, my youngest sister was born, Shauna; she was a beautiful little baby girl.

Mom was having a lot of problems with Shauna's birth, before and after Shauna was born. I can't remember exactly what it was; the doctor ran a few tests, and Mom soon decided to have a hysterectomy. This was a Catholic hospital, so it had to be life threatening for them to do this operation. With Dad not keeping a job for long, Mom now taking care of three kids; the last time Mom and Dad split we all moved in with Grandma. Mom needed help; Dad didn't seem to want to, couldn't, or didn't know how. Mom and Grandma said that he was just another worthless man. "Yeah, a man is only good for just one thing; most of the time they can't even do that right," Grandma and Mom would say all the time. As a child, I didn't know what they meant—I knew it wasn't good.

Dad's brother John and his wife Betty loved children, and they never had any themselves. Uncle John knew that Dad was having financial problems and wanted to help him. So right before school would start, I would spend a weekend with them; they would buy most of my school clothes to get me ready for school. This was a good time for me. I was the one and only. I was getting all of the attention, and I was eating it up.

Most of the time they would take me to the State Fair for the day; one time they took me to a rodeo.

This year was one of those special years where I was going to my first rodeo at Madison Square Gardens; this was a very awesome trip. I can still remember how super excited that I was at the time. I even saw one of my heroes of the day; he was in a lot of the old Westerns back then. I even shook his hand as he went by on his horse around the grandstands. I was so excited I about wet all over myself. (I didn't, but that's how happy I was at the time.) This rodeo was really awesome, all but one part that happened to one of the clowns. They had clowns on the field that when the cowboys would get thrown from their wild horse or bull, the clowns would rush out to get the animal's attention while the cowboy got to safety. These clowns would jump in barrels; the bull would hit the barrel and send the barrel flying.

How the clowns ever survived I never knew. Well, this day one of the clowns did get hurt, and he was rushed to the hospital. I was crying at first, hoping the clown wasn't dead, that he would be all right. My aunt and uncle said that he would be okay, not to worry. They tried to keep my spirits up by telling me that all was going to be okay.

By the end of the rodeo, I was worn out from all of the excitement, hollering and cheering. I was ready for a nap on the way home.

I couldn't wait to get home to tell my family all about the rodeo. I asked my aunt and uncle a few times about the clown. They said that as soon as they found out anything about him that they would let me know. Needless to say it seemed to take forever to get home. I was an excited little boy who just had one of the most awesome days of my whole entire life, and I wanted to share it with my family.

When we pulled up in front of the house, I was up and out of the car and running inside the house going on and on about my trip. I was talking to my sisters, telling them about the bull and the clown that got hurt, when I heard my Mom say:

"Your sisters don't want to hear about all that crap, so be quiet."

"But Mom—" I tried to say.

"We'll talk about this after your aunt and uncle leave, so shut up for now," Mom insisted.

I felt that something was wrong; even some children can sense when something is just not right on the home front. "Mom, what's wrong?" I asked.

"I will tell you later," Mom snapped at me. I noticed that Dad wasn't home.

"Where's Dad? Is he still at work?" I asked. No answer, because my uncle and aunt were coming in the house, laden down with all of my stuff for school and from the trip. Mom and Grandma put on the "Happy Faces" while my aunt and uncle were there. Mom asked if they wanted some coffee, to sit and talk for a spell.

"No, it's late and we have to get back home yet; it's been a really long day," my uncle explained. So they briefly explained how things went, and then they left to go home.

As soon as they left, I asked again: "Mom, where's Dad? He's coming home, right?"

"You know out of all the bullshit your father has put us through and you always act this way when you don't see him," Mom said angrily.

"He's gone again, right?" I said sadly.

"Yes the damn drunk is gone," Grandma yelled. "I kicked him out of here for the last time."

"What…what happened?" I asked sadly.

"Your drunken', NO-good father came home yet once again and he was smashed; he was very verbally mean, and he began to threaten your Mom, and I demanded him to leave," Grandma said. "He then came at me. I went to the phone and called the police. I then told him to get his — off my property or I will have him arrested," Grandma explained, very upset, with tears in her eyes.

"We went through all of this and all you do is ask about your dad," Mom said. "I ought to send you with your drunken' dad since you love him so much."

"Mom—" I tried to say.

"It's late—get ready for bed," Mom told me. I felt so sad. I had such an awesome weekend, beautiful trip with my aunt and uncle, all excited to share all of this with my family, and I couldn't. Instead, I was very saddened about my dad; even with all that we have gone through he was still my Dad, and I loved him. I had a mom and a dad like all the other kids; I wanted to be like every other kid—with parents. I began feeling that some of this was my fault. If I would have stayed home and not out and about all over the place, Dad would still be with us. I wasn't there to stop the fight, and now he's gone. I didn't know where he was; Mom and Grandma said that they didn't know and didn't care.

My sisters, nor I, had seen our Dad for some time. I think he did call a few times, but Grandma and Mom would hang up on him. They said that they have had enough of all Dad's bullshit and they were not going to take anymore. Many a time, Mom or Grandma would turn to me and say: "And if you grow up to be like your dead beat dad, I will disown you too." This was something nice to tell a child.

This year I started in the third grade, which I really didn't like at all. The teacher was very nice; I just wasn't into school at all. I was having problems at school, I was not focusing on my work, and I had no one to really help me when I got home with my schoolwork. At home it was kind of like a war zone. Grandma and Mom would be arguing about something; if Dad called, I would hear a couple of hours of how no good he was. It was sad looking back. Then it happened: Mom and Dad were getting a divorce. I was devastated. I didn't see my dad hardly ever now; now they were getting a divorce? I cried and cried about this. I pleaded with Mom not to leave Dad. The more I would plead with her the angrier she became with me. "I am divorcing your dad because he has not one time stepped up to be a father to you kids, not once," Mom said sternly.

"I am tired of his no-good, worthless self doing nothing but drinking, disrupting this whole family, and not taking the responsibility of raising a family. Why are you so upset and hellbent on holding onto your damn father, after all the beatings that he has given you? All of the broken promises he has failed to keep with you. He has hardly ever been there for you, but he's up at that damn tavern with his buddies," Mom ranted on.

"Mom, if I promise to be good, would you and Dad get back together?" I said to Mom, as she then looked at me and said, "This has nothing to do with you kids at all, it's all about your—" Mom started to say.

"I know that when I'm bad you all get angry at each other and start to fight. I'm sorry, Mom. I'll be good," I insisted through my tears.

"Baby..." Mom said as she brought me close to her as she hugged me. "This has nothing to do with you at all. Damn your drunken' father, damn him for tearing up this family," Mom replied as she hugged me tightly, through our tears and pain. I still believed in my little mind that if I were just a better kid that none of this would be happening.

The divorce, problems at school, I was also very sick with some of the old childhood health problems (chicken pox, mumps, measles, you name it. I seemed to catch it so easily). A couple of good things: Dad did move just a few blocks away from us. Mom said that I could go over to visit him whenever I wanted to. Also, Dad did come over every now and then to help with me during the times that I was sick. Still, I was going through a very traumatic event in my life. I felt that I was the only kid in the whole wide world without a dad at home. I withdrew even more at school; I had very few friends anyway; the teacher almost had to make me get involved in different games. I wanted to be left alone. With missing all of the school that I did, along with the depression I was suffering, I had done lousy in school, and I flunked the third grade. This really helped my self-worth and self-esteem at that time. This was just something else that Mom and Grandma blamed Dad for and how all of this was his fault.

At this time Grandma did not have a shower or tub in the bathroom, so Mom bathed us kids in the sink in the kitchen. My sisters were small enough that Mom bathed them in the sink.

Mom bathed me—at eight, going on nine years old by now—right there in the kitchen. She would bathe me all over, but when it got to my private areas she told me to wash them really good, as she watched me. Many times I would be washing myself and Mom would make fun of how small my penis was, and she would laugh at me. This happened on a few occasions, and I felt so embarrassed and very self-conscious of my privates.

Mother was even more overprotective of me after the divorce than she ever was before. I could not go across the street to play with the neighbor kids. "No, I don't want you to get hurt. I don't have the money to pay for hospital bills," Mom would say. (This was before the insurance of today.) None of the neighbor kids could come over to my house to play: "No one comes over here neither. I don't have the money to pay for anyone getting hurt out there. You have your sisters, go play with them," Mom would say all of the time. A few times one of my school friends who lived right across the street came over and asked if I could come out to play, Mom got angry and sent him home. I got so angry with Mom and Grandma for not letting me have friends over; all I could do is stuff this anger. I also began to dislike my sisters as well; all I was allowed to play with was them, females surrounded me.

I had little to no adult male supervision at all. There were times that I was excited about a home run or something I made when playing ball at school, to just having a good day at school. I would come home and talk about it, and Mom would say: "I'm sending you to school to learn, not to do all of that damn playing. You better bring them damn grades up, boy, or I'm going to beat you." Teachers want me to get more involved in school activities, and Mom said to focus on schoolwork.

I didn't feel accepted by my peers. I wanted to have friends, but I couldn't have them. Mom said schoolwork was all that counted.

As far as I can remember I was always fat; some of the kids at school would make fun of me for being so fat. Before a ball game the teacher picked a couple of team captains, then these guys would pick the kids they wanted on their teams. I was one of the ones that was hardly ever chosen. This hurt, this hurt a lot. I didn't know what to do about it. I wanted to cry and go home, but I didn't. "Come on, I'll take him," one of the guys would say in disgust. All I wanted even back then was to be accepted, feel wanted. I wanted to feel like I belonged somewhere. I never did have that feeling. Most of the time it seemed that I was laughed at, ridiculed, and made fun of—bullied a lot. Another thing that I disliked about myself then was Mom made me have a crewcut haircut, which is how I wear my hair today mostly. (This is a very close cut one looks almost bald really.) So there was a time that when I was in class the kid sitting behind me would flip my ears when the teacher would have her back towards us, and the class would giggle. I would turn around and give him a dirty look he would just laugh. A couple of times I yelled out: "Stop!" only to get in trouble myself. I would be so angry. A few times I came home and told Grandma or Mom. Mom just said: "Say something to the teacher about it, that's what they are there for."

"I have, Mom, and I got in trouble instead."

"Boy, you get yourself in trouble and I have to lose a day's work to go to that school I will half kill you when I get you home, you hear me, boy?"

"Yes, Mom," I said, very disappointingly.

I felt that I had no one to talk to, about anything really. The problems at school, with most of my peers, did not get any better. I was feeling so worthless, helpless, and all alone. Even though I was not the only one my peers chose to pick on and made fun of, I felt like it was most of the time.

Dad soon moved into a house just a couple of blocks away from where we lived. It was pretty cool at first. I was able to go over and visit him from time to time. I was able to hang out with him. I soon was not feeling that loss, that void of Dad not being at the house. Of course, over time, things changed. I would go over to visit, and Dad would not come to the door. Later, I found out he was taking a nap; Mom said that he was just sleeping off a drunk. Or I would call him to talk to him and he wouldn't be home or he was asleep or something, then the rejection began to set in even more. I wanted to spend time with my dad so badly, and he seemed not to have the time for me. He was either with his buddies at a tavern or taking a nap.

Dad liked to go fishing and so did I. We did go fishing every now and then.

As soon as we got back in town, we would stop at one of the taverns that Dad went to all the time. Which at the time I thought it was cool. I was hanging out with my Dad. I was at a tavern with him. He would buy me a soda or two, depending on how long he was going to stay. Then he would take me home, and I would spend the next hour explaining all of the fun that Dad and I had fishing. (Which never went over very good with Mom or Grandma.)

During these early stages of my life, I went through a lot of physical, mental, psychological, and some sexual abuse.

My mom and grandma took the "Spare the Rod, Spoil The Child" literally; so did my Dad. It seemed like my sisters got away with almost everything and I was the "whipping boy." My dad was an alcoholic; I felt he betrayed me, his whole family, really. I had little-to-no male bounding at all in my life. Dad did spend some time with me, but a lot of it was in a tavern or visiting him with him drinking at his house. There was no real male adult for me to look up to or seek real direction. My Uncle John was one I could trust and share with, but he lived forty to fifty miles away, and I hardly ever saw him. Mom's brother was not around hardly either; we would go to visit his family every now and then. They would all come over to visit Grandma, very seldom. I was able to spend a little time with him, but my uncle was a major control freak, dominant and demanding. (All of which reminded me of Mom.)

Mom and Grandma seemed to hate most men so much, because of their past experiences. I mostly heard how disgusting men were, how worthless and useless we were, along with all of the threats of "I better not grow up like my dad."

This done little for my self-worth and self-esteem. I grew up knowing just how worthless men were—to most women.

When Dad and Mom got their divorce Dad was supposed to pay child support. It was difficult to get money from Dad when he worked; we still had to be fed in the wintertime as well. Mom worked and made a little, Grandma was getting Social Security, plus doing some babysitting on the side; things were very tight. There was no public aide back then like there is now. There was a truck that came to the city hall once a month to hand out some government commodities, that was all. Dad had to get this money from somewhere to feed his family. Dad was supposed to pay Mom this money every Friday or Saturday. Dad was to come by, pick Mom up, and take her to the store to buy groceries and then bring her home. It seemed rarely to be this easy for some reason.

At first Mom had to call a number of the taverns in town to see where Dad was at. Once she found him, she had to let him know that she was ready to go to the store. After a while Dad finally came to pick Mom up; he then took her to the store, dropped Mom off, and then went back to the tavern. Needless to say, this made Mom very angry because then she would have to track him down again. (Sorry—no cell phones at this time either.) Soon Mom had me to do this entire calling. When I could not find him she told me to get on my bicycle and go downtown to get Dad out of one of those damn taverns, that Mom needed to go shopping—NOW. There would be times that I would just miss Dad at the tavern that I went to. I would end up finding him at home, just lying down for a nap. Then I would have to tell Mom that Dad would be over after he got up from his nap. Mom would rant and rave the whole time almost until Dad finally pulls up out front to pick Mom up. I learned at a very early age how to "butter up both sides of the bread." When I found Dad I would explain a candy-coated story to try to get him to want to pick Mom up sooner than later.

Then I would candy coat things to Mom about what Dad said so she would stop exploding all over me, for doing what she told me to do. I loved both of my parents, but there were times that I wanted to just run away from home. There were times that I wanted to hurt them so bad; these were adults acting like a bunch of kids, and they pulled me right into the middle of this turmoil.

So I was developing an inner hatred to females in general. I had problems with my sisters; at times I could not stand them either. It showed through all of the fights that I picked with them in our childhood, which led to most of the beatings that I received.

Then when I did begin to notice girls in school, Mom went bonkers. She went on and on about how I was just like a man, how I was just like my Dad. How that girl was not good enough for me. "All girls want to do is to take you for everything that you got and then they kick you to the curb," Mom would say. All of this and more I heard almost every day; these tapes were so engrained in my memory, I played them so much I began to believe them. I could not think of another thing that was as worthless and good for nothing than a "man," my dad especially, all men generally speaking, according to Mom and Grandma.

This one day I was sitting on the couch in the front room, next to my sister Shauna. Grandma and Shauna got into an argument about something. Shauna began to cuss Grandma. I backhanded her in the mouth and busted her lip open and she was bleeding badly at first. When Grandma got the blood to stop and got Shauna all cleaned up, Shauna ran over and told Dad what I had done. (Another day in my life that is as clear as it happened yesterday.) The next thing I know, Dad was racing around the corner in his car. He came to a screeching stop in front of the house. He got out of the car, and he came into the house without knocking like he normally does and came straight over to me with anger and rage in his eyes that I have not seen for some time. He yelled at me: "I thought that I told you to never touch these girls again!" as he slapped my face.

"But Dad, let me explain—" I tried to say, as he began to take off his belt.

"Boy, I'm going to teach you a lesson, and if you ever touch these girls again, I'll kill you," Dad said as he began to swing his belt at me and hit me all over my body.

Somehow, I broke away, and I ran into the kitchen. Dad was right behind me, swinging all the way. I'm hurting and hurting bad. I fell down next to this cabinet in the kitchen, and here was where he then began to beat me with his fists.

Grandma then yelled at Dad: "Stop, that's enough!" Dad kept pounding away it seemed. "If you do not stop I will have to call the police!" Grandma yelled.

"I'm tired of this damn kid not listening to me nor his mother. He will do as I say or I will—" Dad started to say as he gave me a couple of kicks.

"You need to stop NOW!" Grandma insisted.

"Only punks pick on defenseless little girls. Never touch them again, you hear me, BOY!" Dad yelled at me inches from my face.

"Yes!" I cried. I was in a fetal position, with my arms covering my head and face, trying to protect myself the best that I could from Dad's fists and his kicks. Dad gave me a couple of kicks and then went back to the front room. Grandma then hung the phone up as Dad walked into the front room and sat down. Once Dad began to calm down a little, Grandma began to explain what started everything. Which really didn't mean much to Dad, it seemed.

Dad soon left, and I went into my bedroom and cried. This was just another time that I got a beaten because of my sisters (not for what I had done...?). I was angry with my sisters, angry with my dad for what he done to me. I hated them, and I wanted to hurt them all. Then when Mom came home from work, she was not happy with me either. She saw some of my bruises. I got a verbal tongue lashing, but that is all, surprisingly. Even after this day I still had problems with my sisters on and off. Most people would think of this as just sibling rivalry. At those times I really wanted to hurt them, revenge. I was filled with anger and hatred at those times. Every time that I got a beaten from Mom or Dad, the more I could not stand my sisters at that time.

My mom had kept a tight grip on me; she controlled my every move almost. I look outside and I saw the neighbor kids out playing and having fun, running, jumping and playing different games. The times that I was really touched is when I saw their dads outside playing with them. How I longed to have these things growing up.

All of this filtered through to school and to my peers; many times I was made fun of, called a Mama's boy, a wimp, a fat bowling ball. Things got to the point that I got some attention from my peers when I made fun of myself and cut myself down in front of them. I got a chuckle; they laughed and just shook their heads and went on. There I stood, feeling like a laughingstock of the playground.

I believe that I was in the fifth grade when I began to notice girls. I told myself that all girls were not brats like my sisters and they were okay. Back then, there was a thing called "Going Steady." This was when a boy saw a girl that he liked and he hung out with her. You would see different ones holding hands. They were really good friends, girlfriend and boyfriend. I heard of this "rite of passage" thing "Going Steady," but I didn't know how to do it. I didn't know what I was supposed to do once a girl says yes to go steady. So I watched some of the other kids on the playground how they did it and the things that they did when they are going study

At eleven years old I did not know a thing about "Clicks," "Groups," or even "Gangs." I knew about rejection, some of the pain that bullies dished out, but being laughed at by peer girls was the ultimate form of rejection; here I got a very rude awakening. "No, man, are you crazy?" one girl said, as she snubbed me and walked off with her friends.

I asked this one girl, her name was Patty. She seemed to be a real nice girl; she had a lot of friends. She was seen laughing, joking, and was very popular. I began to have a crush on her and wanted to be her friend too. One day I got bold enough to ask her if she would like to go steady with me. The other girls tried to hold back their outburst of laughter, as Patty politely told me that she was already going steady with someone. She thanked me for asking her though. I was so embarrassed and disappointed at her saying no. Some of the deeper, real hurt came each time I passed these girls; after that, I thought that I was being laughed at.

One day I noticed this girl, Mary. I saw her by herself a lot, just like me. She kind of reminded me of myself. I was really feeling devastated from the other girls and how I was treated. I was extremely shy over taking on more rejection at this time. Testing the waters, I would go by her from time to time to see if she noticed me; I would smile, and so would she. She than hung her head in embarrassment, like I do. Then I would speed up and walk the other way.

One day I walked up to her, and we started talking; we talked about school, how hard some of the work was we were doing, just kid things. Each day that I went to school I looked for Mary, and we walked around the playground and we started playing different ball games, just hanging out and having fun. I was feeling kind of funny on the inside of me, it was a good funny, and I didn't know what it was at that time. I started to feel real good while I was around Mary. I was telling myself that this is how it feels when you like a girl, this is how you feel before you ask the girl to go steady.

"Go steady! I'm going to ask Mary to go steady with me," I said to myself one day.

I got home from school this day and I was all excited about Mary: "Grandma, I met this girl at school, and she is really cool," I began to say all excited and happy.

Grandma smiled and said: "Boy, wait till your Mom gets home and tell her about all of this."

"I will—" as I go on and on how good I feel, how happy I feel when I'm around her, how we hang out all the time on the playground. Grandma didn't say much of anything other than something called "Puppy Love." "'Puppy Love,' that's all it is, you'll get over it soon." When Mom got home from work I was all excited to tell her about Mary. Mom was very angry with me.

"I send you to school to learn and not mess with girls!" she yelled. "All them damn girls want is to get whatever they can from you and that's it. They are no good.

"You do your schoolwork and leave those damn girls alone," Mom demanded looking at me, staring me down. "Do you understand me?"

"But Mom…the other guys—" I tried to say.

Mom sat on the edge of the couch, looked at me very seriously, and said, "I don't give a damn about anyone but you. You go to school, learn, and leave those damn girls alone, understand?"

"Yes, ma'am," I said.

"Good. I don't want to hear any more about these damn girls. Do you have your homework done?"

"No, ma'am," I said.

"Just like your damn dad, never does a damn thing he is supposed to do. Get the shit done and then you go to bed," Mom demanded. I was very upset that Mom didn't like this idea at all; it was school, school, school and that's all. I went to school the next day, and I got up the nerve to ask Mary the question: "Mary, would you go steady with me?" I was scared, I was nervous; I was shaking in my shoes.

Mary thought for a minute, she smiled, and then lowered her head: "Yeah, I guess so," Mary said modestly.

"Really?" shocked and surprised I said. "I mean, okay, great, sounds good, thanks."

"Now what?" I said to myself. As I stood there in front of her, smiling too and not knowing what to do next.

Then she looked at me with a puzzled look and I asked: "What's wrong?"

"Do you have a ring or something you want me to hold on to, that says I'm going with you?" "Yes, I got it at home. I'll bring it this afternoon after lunch," I explained. She smiled then and reached out her hand to me and we walked over to the jungle gym and climbed around for a while. I was the happiest kid in the world that time.

At noon I went home for lunch. There, Grandma would have lunch all waiting for me when I got there. Grandma asked me about the girl at school and I told her how beautiful she was and how much I liked her. "You know what your mom said," Grandma reminded me.

"Yes, Grandma, schoolwork, I know," I replied.

After lunch Grandma was busy cleaning up and I went to Mom's bedroom (also my room), and I went to Mom's jewelry box looking for a ring that I could give Mary like I promised her.

Mom had tons of different rings, necklaces, pins, and earrings. "Mom will never miss one little ring," I told myself, knowing that this would be my death sentence if I were caught. I saw this one ring that had two little hearts on it. I grabbed it and put it in my pocket and slowly closed the lid of the jewelry box. As I came out of the room, I looked at the clock, and it was almost time to go back to school. "Grandma, I better get going. It's almost time to get back to school," I said.

"See you later," Grandma said. I got down the street a little ways and I looked at the ring again. I could not believe that I had the guts to steal one of my mom's rings. When she finds out she will kill me, really kill me. One time I stole a quarter from Grandma, I got the beaten of my life; this would be sure death for me.

When I got to school, I looked for Mary. When we saw each other we smiled and were happy to see each other. "Well?" she asked.

"Well what?" I said in a puzzled voice. Mary looked sad, as she put her hands on her hips and just stood there.

"Oh, you mean this?" I said as I reached into my pocket and pulled out the ring.

Mary took the ring and put it on, then said: "Thanks, this is a real ring—

most of the other girls got a ring out of a bubble gum machine. Here I got a real ring," Mary said as she leaned over and kissed me on my cheek. That kiss felt funny, a good funny, as I reached up to touch my cheek that she just kissed. I must have had a weird look on my face, because Mary asked: "You okay?"

"Yeah, I think so," I said.

"Good. Come on, I want to show some of the other girls," Mary said. As she took me by the hand and she led me all around to her friends, showing off the ring that I just gave her. I was so embarrassed at first, then I really didn't care; if Mom found out these would be my last days on earth.

All I wanted is to be like the other kids. I wanted to be and feel normal; however, that was at the time. I wanted to be part of things and not the focus of bullies and terrible jokes. I wanted to be a kid, just a normal kid, that's all.

Needless to say, this "Puppy Love" thing that Grandma was talking about, she was right, I think it might lasted a few weeks, and I lost interest in Mary, and all girls really.

It was a long time later Mom was looking for that ring. She was asking Grandma about it one day. Grandma said: "How did you ever notice that the ring was gone with all of the stuff that you have in that box?"

"Mom, you know me, you know I can tell when something is missing and someone was in my jewelry box," Mom said as she came out of her room looking at us in the kitchen. I could have sworn that she was looking right at me.

"I don't know, Mom," us three kids chimed together.

My bed was also in my mom's bedroom. I had my own bed, but I did not always sleep in it. There were times that Mom had me sleep in her bed as well. I didn't like this that much, but I did what I was told to do. This one night I remembered waking up in the middle of the night. I was gasping for my breath. I opened my eyes and I saw these huge breasts right above my face. Mom was lifting off the top of me saying: "I'm sorry, I'm sorry, are you okay?"

"Yeah, I guess," I said as I rolled over and went back to sleep. I was in Mom's bed at different times until I was thirteen or fourteen, I believe. That's all that I remembered—or wanted to remember.

Soon I was in junior high school, and boy, I thought I was something, I was growing up, and I'm in the big time now. I have many different classes, different teachers, and a locker in the hall to put all of my books. Didn't have recess anymore, but we did have a PE class, which I hated from the very first day. One of the main reasons is that you had to undress in front of all these strange guys, run yourself to death almost all hour, then—then you had to take a shower. That meant undressing and going naked into the shower with all these guys I didn't know from Adam. I was scared to death to take a shower, knowing that everyone will make fun of me, call me names. I was so embarrassed. One day the coach caught me not taking a shower and he told me to get undressed and take a shower—"NOW!!" were his words. I was even more embarrassed now, because most of the other guys were dressing and I was just going to the showers—naked. I heard a number of chuckles as I cautiously walked into the shower. Not much was said that day, because the coach was still in the room, but some of the other days some of the guys looked at me, laughed at me how small I was, how they couldn't see anything. Where was —; who chopped it off? Was I really a guy or—?" As they laughed and made fun of me.

Some of them asked if I was a girl or boy, maybe I was one of those freaks; I had female parts but a male body. (Not much talk about transgender at this time.) I was so hurt, offended, scared, upset, and just wanted to run away. I also felt very angry and wanted to lash out and hurt these guys every time they verbally hurt me like that. "Man, you can never satisfy a girl—" one kid would say, and half the room seems to erupt into laughter. I would quickly dry off and get dressed. I suffered this ridicule allot all the way through high school as well. All of those sick tapes played over and over in my head through my entire life.

This harassment got too much at this one point; I tried to tell the coach about it. All he would say: "Grow up. Stop being a mama's boy. Don't let that crap bother you like that. Go on get out of here and get to your next class." I was scared to death to say anything to Mom about this, because she has said the same thing about my privates. If I said anything to Dad about this, he would say something to Mom. I would really get in trouble then. So I chose to just skip gym; at gym time I would leave school and walk into town to eat lunch, and then go back to school to finish the school day. This seemed to be working out pretty good, until after the first of the year; some of our classes got changed around, and I ended up having my coach for last hour study hall. Oh boy, I was in serious, deep trouble now. At one point in the study hall the coach stopped by and asked me how I was feeling. Kind of puzzled, I said, "Okay."

"I would like to talk to you after class," he said.

"Yes, sir," I said as I was trembling. He patted me on the shoulder and walked on. After the bell rang at the end of the class and all the kids left, I walked up to the coach. He asked: "Mister, I haven't seen you… in how long?"

"It's been a while, sir," I replied.

"Where have you been, young man?"

"I wasn't able to take PE, so I went to town for lunch and then I came back for the rest—" I tried to explain.

"So do you have a doctor's excuse for all of this time that you have missed PE?"

"Yes, sir," I said as I lied through my teeth.

"Good. I would like to see it tomorrow when you come back to PE," the coach said very seriously, calmly, and respectfully.

"Yes, sir," I said.

"Good. That will be all, sir. I will see you tomorrow."

I missed the bus. I had to walk over a couple of miles home. Boy, was I going to get in deep trouble. I lied big time to the coach, I lied big time when I got home. I said something like I had to go to the bathroom real bad and that's why I missed the bus. (No cell phones.) I did not have a doctor's excuse, of course. Now what was I going to do? I was scared of getting in trouble at school. The school would want to see Mom and then she would kill me for getting in trouble and for having to miss work. I would get my butt beat by the principal for lying and skipping class. I was so scared I didn't know what to do. (Corporal Punishment was still practiced at this time.) One would think, when all else fails, you get your "hand caught in the cookie jar," you fess up, tell the truth, and take your consequences like a man and move on—right? Not me. I thought up a scheme that I knew was going to get me off the hook. I sat down and wrote a *letter*, yes, a **letter**, supposedly from my doctor explaining why I have missed PE for the past two months. I really laid it on in this letter. I did my best to cover all my bases in this letter. I thought it was very good myself. When I went to school the next day, I had one of my friends sign my doctor's name to the letter. I then took this to the office and asked them to put this in the coach's mailbox.

Thinking that this letter would explain it all. I didn't go to PE that day either. I was thinking about skipping last hour study hall, but I didn't. I went to my study hall feeling pretty good about myself, because I see the coach in the hall a few times throughout the day and he never said a word to me. Boy, was I fooled. This one time as the coach was making his rounds through the room, he stopped by me and said: "Mister, I will need to see you after class."

"Yes, sir," was all that I could say. When that last bell rang, I think my heart stopped for a second; I got very nervous and scared, even more than I was already. After the room cleared out the coach came over to me with the letter in his hand. "This is a very good letter, mister," the coach said.

"Sir?"

"Be careful, mister, when you answer my next question. Your answer will determine everything that will happen there after. Do you understand me?" the coach said very seriously.

"Y-E-S, sir?" I said, and I knew I was in deep trouble.

"I do not want ANY of your BS. I do not want nor will I accept any lies whatsoever. Do you fully hear me and understand me?"

"Yes, sir," I replied, trembling in my seat.

"Now," as he tossed the letter on the table in front of me, "who wrote this, and who signed that name to this? I want the truth right NOW!"

I was shaking with fear as I stuttered and said: "I…did, s-s-sir."

"Now, for those two months then you just skipped PE and went downtown, you said, then came back to school, is that correct?" the coach said. "So that part of your story was true?" he asked.

"Yes, sir," I replied, hanging my head.

"Why, why did you feel that you had to skip two whole months of class, fail this course, and not once think you were going to get caught?"

"I told you—" I tried to say.

"What did you try to tell me and when?" the coach said angrily

"Over three months ago, sir. I told you how a lot of the kids were teasing me and making fun of me all of the time when I take my shower. Then all of the running we were doing everyday—it was just too much. I can't run that good, and I had to stop and walk, and this just got the guys to make fun of me even more," I explained, through my fear, with tears in my eyes.

"Boy, that's life, some people make fun of others. I told you then to grow up and not let this crap bother you," the coach insisted. "Do your parents know about any of this?" the coach asked.

"My dad doesn't care, and my mom would kill me if she knew," I said as I began to shake even more.

"What am I to do, mister? I have to do something here," the coach said. "I just can't have guys skipping classes whenever they like and not do anything about it." I just sat there and waited for my punishment, as the Coach thought of what he was going to do with me. "Mister, you have two choices, here they are: A.) You and I will go into the office, we will explain all of this to the principal, who then will call your dad and mom to come in and we will take care of this then." I was trembling in fear, with a tear flowing down my face. "B.) You give me your solemn promise that you will not miss one gym class for the rest of the school year. That you will dress out and take full part in every class and you will shower after every class. If you have any more problems in my class, I want you to come to me and talk to me. Don't ever try this crap with me again," the coach said as he picked up my letter. "Do we fully understand each other?" the coach said very sternly.

"Yes, sir," I said.

"That's all, mister. I will see you in gym class tomorrow, right?!"

"Yes, sir," I said as I stood up, collected my books. I was confused on what was going to happen to me. This must have showed in my behavior because the coach asked: "Is there a problem, mister?"

"Sir…" I started to say.

"Sir, all I want to here from you, if anything, is an 'I'm sorry,' and that's all, sir, then you may go," the coach said quite clearly.

"Yes, sir. I'm sorry, sir," I said.

"Good. Now you may go. Get out of here before I change my mind," the coach demanded. I left as quickly as I could. You bet I did not miss one class, and if for some reason that I didn't or couldn't dress out, I did have an excuse from Mom or Grandma; this was not very often. The coach did talk to the whole class about the problem of making fun of others, and I had very few problems after that. This didn't happen just to me; others were made fun of too.

Kids bullying others was a big thing even back in the '60s and '70s; it was a fact of life you had to deal with it, as unpleasant as all of this was—for the bullied person, of course. Another life-changing experience for me during this time was I began to notice I had an attraction to some of the guys. This had to be one of the worst things in life was homosexuality, in this time era; it was looked at then with that disgust, fear, hatred, and anger as pedophilia is today.

I had this secret desire for some of the males that I had seen at school, then when I saw them in gym class, I had to really watch myself as not to show this, or I would face even more problems. This pain, confusion, even self-hatred, low self-worth and self-esteem, along with bouts of depression, did not help me at all during this time. Not knowing what to do. Not knowing who I could trust to talk to. All I chose to do is stuff these hideous, disgusting thoughts and feelings and put on the facade of "normalcy" the best I could, whatever "normal" is? (Of course, this was not the healthy way to handle things; this didn't work for my dad and I saw how it was affecting him.)

Bombarded with "old tapes" in my head from Mom: "All men are good for only one thing and fail at that most of the time," "You better not turn out like your drunken good-for-nothing dad!" "ALL girls want to do is use you and take you for all they can." "No sex before marriage!" "Respect her and don't get her pregnant, then decide to marry her; that is the very wrong thing to do."

This was just a small sample of the things told to me by Mom, then add in the many confusing things other people, peers, family and society alike have instilled into this young mind, it can be baffling to most anyone. Being a teenager is challenging; having all these questions with no answers is not healthy as well.

Note: I know in our society there are people that have gone or are going through allot worse than I ever have and made better choices for their lives. God bless you all! I also know that there are millions of more lives that are still suffering from years of abuse and are still suffering on into their adulthood.

There is *hope* for all victims. For me and numerous other people, it has taken years of therapy and lots of very hard work, very deep soul searching, and self-introspection.

It's time to take full control of your life; our past does not have to dictate the rest of our lives. The path to becoming a survivor is knowing your past and managing the rest of your life the best you can.

Stage II
Set Up
Grooming To Assaults

NOTE: This book was solely written as a learning/teaching aide about one of society's deepest, darkest cultural behavioral monsters. Little has been written on this "Closet Monster," for very good reasons, but the "Out of Sight, Out of Mind" mentality has led us to an epidemic that our society has today. Pedophilia is so hideous, so devastating to all victims/their families as well— for their whole life—to one degree or another. Pedophilia is nothing new; it's really been around since the beginning of time. It has been called many different things across many cultural divides and justified in many different ways, all fitting for that time period. Most are handled in the same way— pushed deep into the closet where other skeletons are kept, covered with deep doses of denial, hoping that it will all soon go away. Then when something does happen, "Why, God, WHY!" Of course, there is no reason, NO justifications to why. Education, learning knowledge is power will be the only way to help the victims, and yes, the predators as well.

In this following chapter, "Set Up: Grooming to Assaults" are some of the ways that a predator may choose to act out. Here again I want to point out that the environment, the family, friends, or the lack of friends, did not make the predators do any of the things that the predators chose to do. Those were their choices and their choices alone.

IF you are a victim and choose not to become a predator; God bless you. Please, if you are having deep issues with any of those things, please seek help ASAP. This hell doesn't need to ruin your entire life any longer. Stuffing all that pain, anger, rage, and self-deprivation is some of what is stopping you from enjoying the rest of your life.

No one can change their past; you do have control over the here and now—your future.

Our society is made up of way too many single-parent families, may it be a mom as head of household, or may it be a dad.

Or you have a very kind and loving family where one or both parents have full-time jobs where one or both parents are busy working and paying bills, and now they have mostly "Latch-Key Kids," where the older children are helping to raise their younger brothers and sisters. Children helping to raise children? Sad but true, and this does happen way too often even within our society of the day. Both parents feel guilty about this, but daycare or having and adult sitter would eat up most if not all of one of their incomes. So the parents are forced to choose the less of two situations, trusting their older, responsible children to care for their younger siblings while the adults have to work. The pros and cons of this could be too numerous to mention. This happens, it's life; in most cases, the family learns to make the adjustments and grow with it. Other families will need to seek other options.

One of the most important things to always remember is to let your children know just how much you LOVE them and how special that they are to you, to the family. Let them know that they are loved and accepted for them and not as a slave to the family. Don't say, "We all have a job to do in this family, step up and become an adult," when they are just a child needing your love and support.

This is so important for them to know that you love them. It's not so much to do with the *quantity* of time with your children, but the *quality* of that time. Whatever the amount of time one spends with their family, do your best to make it as positive, memorable, loving, and caring as possible. I know that this can be very difficult with the parent(s) working full-time jobs, then coming home from having a rough day and wanting to spend quality time with their family...? *Please!*

I'm not saying this to scare you or your family.

If you do not take the time to show **your** children that they are **loved**, that you **care** for them and are concerned for their wellbeing, "*someone else soon will!*"

Which brings us to the next phase, set pp/grooming to assaults of the potential victim.

Set Up/Grooming

To begin with I need to point out that there are millions of adults that truly love children and are helping, guiding, and are very good mentors. These people are truly unsung heroes that need our positive recognition. It is the "Wolves In Sheeps' Clothing" that one needs to be aware of at anytime. Most of the time it is very difficult to notice the difference, knowing your child is the most important and your most valuable person in your life. Also know that some children can be very moody and go through many behavioral changes. This is why it is vital to know your child, and when you have questions about certain types of changes in their behavior, stop and talk to them to see what may be going on—if anything. You are wanting your child to know that they are cared for and loved, not controlled and manipulated. That they can come to you to share anything, good, bad, or questionable that they may be going through to get your guidance, your support, direction, and advice. They need to understand that trust is earned, over time, not just handed out because of their age. "Trust, But Verify" is very good advice, especially if your "parental intuition" is having questionable thoughts and feelings about something or someone in your child's life.

These are very precious people in your lives, and we need to be their best stewards as one can be. I'm not sharing any of these things to scare parents but asking them to be more aware of their precious children.

FYI

> Most predators are very slick, cunning, extremely deceitful, and manipulative. Some could sell snow to an Eskimo and make them feel that they got an awesome deal. The children that are the *most* vulnerable are single-parent families or a family where both parents have jobs and must work to support their families. (Which is a very high percentage of families today.) Worst yet is when a family cannot afford childcare, and they must leave an older, responsible(?) child in charge of their siblings. This is not very wise; it happens way too often, and better options need to be evaluated, for the sake and safety of all the children. ***Most predators are not on any state or federal watchlist***—yet search

these lists if a person may be questionable. (***Caution:*** Not all predators have been caught—yet.)

> Most predators will not just take a child off the streets; most will search, hunt, stalk for a time before even making first contact with a child. That is why they are called predators; they hunt for and prey on the most vulnerable.

> ***Most*** predators are known by the child and even the family. Sadly, most are trusted and loved by the family and are accepted as being a part of that family unit.

> Some predators even live within the same home as the child and are very trusted members of said family.

> Then there are predators that even help the family out financially, becoming a very intricate member of this family. To the point where the family may expect or even becomes dependent on their assistance. (Like an adult willing to supervise your children while you and your spouse work.) There are truly "Good Samaritans," don't get me wrong—please be aware and stay aware of any changes within the family dynamics.

> The children like or may be very close to this family member, and you begin to see one or more of the children have or becoming a little more distant or very close to this person. I would want to know if there was a problem.

> This family member seems to be spending more time and may be giving more attention to one or more of your children than any of the other children. Be aware of this and be aware of any mood or behavioral changes within your child.

> You are seeing your child have money or gifts that you have not given them, like a new bicycle, skateboard, clothes, or other expensive electronics. From whom? Why? For what reason(s)?

Would be questions that I would be asking the child and the person who gave these things to the child. A casual, small gift for a birthday or special family event is one thing; the child having many new things over a course of time would be questionable. Confronting the child in an aggressive, authoritarian manner would be very inconclusive. Asking your child about the gifts, in a non-accusing way, stressing your concern and wanting to know for the best interest of your child *might* render better results.

> Stay aware, that there are male and female predictors of all ages, creeds, nationalities, and socioeconomic levels. That male and female children can be prey. There are more female victims than male; both can be vulnerable at any time.
> Only a fraction of all offenses against children are ever reported.

"Parents Beware!"

If you see or even feel questionable behavioral changes, sit down and have a loving and caring conversation with your child. The issue may be nothing at all. Above all else, the child will see or begin to sense that you care for them and are interested in their wellbeing. Some children may feel like they are being watched, controlled, and manipulated yet again. Do your best to reassure them that you truly love and care for them and don't want them to get hurt.

> All children want is to be loved, accepted for who they are, like most all adults do. Some children if they do not think or feel they have this at home, some will search for it somewhere else. (Consciously or sub-consciously... Willingly or unknowingly)
> The older the child the more freedom they want and will soon expect. Trying to come to a reasonable, responsible, and sensible agreement on this will depend on the trust of your child and what you feel comfortable with at the time. All children are different; they must understand that "trust" is earned and sensible steps taken by the parent(s).
> Please, don't be overprotective or a smothering parent either, for this can be as counterproductive as little to no boundaries. Baby steps to freedom; trust is earned and not just given. Trust is given, and it can be and will be taken away if problems arise.
> Be adamant about your child's achievements, be proud of them. Point out and help them work through all the issues they will have, forgive and move on. Life is too short to lose one valuable moment with grudges and holding past mistakes over them.
> "Spare the rod, spoil the child." In the Bible, the good shepherds used

the rod for guidance, *truly* out of love and care for their flock. Very seldom used it in a beating or discipline, but for protection. How do you use the rod in your family?

I would like to share a few more things to be aware of and help you with keeping your children safe as possible. Not all predators are known by the family, friends of the family, nor relatives; some are way more covert than that. The only thing that can be done in this case is to be aware that these things do happen and teach your children about ***"Stranger Danger."*** Above all else your child must know that they are loved—unconditionally—can talk to you about anything—at any time. They need to know that you love them and will protect them all you can, at any time.

"Stranger Danger"

All children, of any age, can be taught about talking to strangers, being polite and respectful to adults, but to run in the case of danger. Then teaching them the difference between a "Good Touch" and "Bad Touch." The difference between a pat on the back or the touching and/or fondling of their private parts. That they have the perfect right to say "NO!" and to run away from this danger as soon as they can. Then to tell a trusted adult about what happened for their protection. These things need to be taught to your children—casually—during an age-appropriate conversation—from time to time, by the parent(s) and even at school, at any age, boys or girls.

Once you have shared these things with your children and they seem to comprehend, just check in with them from time to time to see how they are doing. A casual "How was your day?" will suffice.

All of these things can be done causally, "matter of factually," and not have to scare your child or have them feel that they have done something wrong. Stop putting this off, stop making excuses to yourself your child is too young or too old for all of this. (Victims' ages can be from newborn to seventeen years of age. To adult victims at any age.) Worse yet, thinking these things don't happen in your community, why alarm your children like this, is a very big mistake. Any excuses that you make could put your child in grave danger.

To make things even more challenging is the most covert predators. See by teaching your children all about "Stranger Danger," along with "Good Touch, Bad Touch"; they will know that if any of the following happens, they must run to safety, as soon as possible. Sadly is when a family member or someone close and respected by the family is in question. The safety of the child is paramount! Find out what information that you can and let the authorities do the rest. Never leave a child in this; get the child and yourself far away from all of this torment as soon as possible.

What I'm about to share with you is some predatory behavior of some predators. Again, FYI and not to scare or alarm anyone.

The Hunt

"The Hunt," "On the Prowl," sounds so sadistic, very predatory, and extremely animalistic; it is very much so. Just like the animals in the wild, some predators will hunt, search, and prowl different neighborhoods, parks, malls, public swimming pools, and other places where children may congregate to find a potential victim. Some may even ask other children about a child they are stalking. To get the child's name, where that child may live. May even ask about the brothers and sisters of that family as well. This is all information they will use to make the child feel more trusting on the predator's first contact. Some predators will watch a child for some time before they even speak to the child for the first time. As soon as the predator is tired of all of these formalities and fantasies, about said child, it will be time to meet this child—personally, cautiously walking through their very premeditated plans that they have acted out in their minds for some time. Taking all of the precautions to have the child feel as safe as possible so the child will not get spooked and run off. The predator may meet and talk with the child a few times before enticing the child to go with them to get ice cream, a burger, etc. Most of the time, when the child doesn't feel any danger they will readily go with this person. (The child may have seen and met this person a few times now, so this person may not be seen as a stranger. This person is giving this child attention, attention that a child craves—they may not be receiving at home—some children will find it somewhere else.). There could be people that have been watching your child and will be more than happy to give this child attention, not the positive, healthy kind that the child may receive at home.

Most predators will not harm the child at this time; most predators are much more cunning and covert than that. Even though the predator has envisioned a number of different scenarios in their minds, they don't feel that the child has trust in them yet. The predator may meet the child's other siblings; eventually they might meet the child's parent(s), depending on what the predator has in mind at the time. The predator might choose more than one of the children or maybe one of the child's friends at the time, as well.

At this time the predator is not only setting the child up, they are painstakingly setting up the whole family. The more trust that the predator gains, over time, then they will slowly begin to wean the child(ren) away from everyone else. The more trust the child will develop, in the predator, sooner they will become a victim.

Most predators will first befriend the child, entice them with personal attention, treating the child as an adult even. As the child develops more trust, then to hold the child's interest the predator will begin to take the child to movies, game rooms, even give the child small gifts, small amounts of money. By this time the predator will know the child's likes and dislikes, the child's "wants" and "needs," and they will begin to fulfill the child's whims as much as they can, when they can. Depending on the child's age this could be clothes, video games, expensive tech toys, watches, cellphones, tablets, yes, even drugs and alcohol, to small, meaningless jobs around the predators' home or apartment could be used to build a fantasy world that the child will soon be engulfed in, ensnared in, and even in some cases scared to leave; worst ever, the child doesn't want to leave. After a period of time, the predator senses he has the child hooked, snagged tightly in their web of deception; the predator will soon make the child their next victim. The predator will feel that they have *invested* enough into the child; the predator now feels that this child owes them, their family owes them; it's time for the predator's reward.

To Assaults

The predator has been planning for this time for quite a while now. All of the fantasies and different scenarios they have played out in their minds a number of times, the predator feels it is time for their just rewards.

Now, most will not just assault the child; the predator has a game for this as well. Which will end up with the child being alone with the predator, for a length of time, totally at the control of the predator and the predator's whim now. The predator does not want to scare the child, for fear the child will tell on them. So the predator's approach here will be as cunning as the whole set up and grooming that they have been doing for a time now. The ruse could be as simply as horseplay around with the child. Depending on the child's age could include drugs, alcohol, card games, XXX movies, anything to get the child to feel as safe as possible before assaulting them.

Over this time period, the child has begun to really trust this predator; the child thinks of this person as a close, trusted friend and would almost do anything for the predator. The child may have grown to love this person—a lot. The predator has set the whole family up for some time, so when the parent(s) gives permission for their child to spend the night or weekend with the predator, there will be little questions or concerns about the child's safety, at that time.

Everything that has happened to this point has been plotted, planned, premeditated, and set up before the first time the predator met the child, in most cases. When the predator begins the assault and the victim rejects them, the predator will do their best to reassure the child that they will like what their wanting to do. That there is nothing wrong with any of these things and to relax. The predator will go as far as enticing the child with promises of gifts, money, whatever to get what the predator wants. Most of the time this will work, and the assault happens.

If the victim would still reject the predator, the predator may become more aggressive. Most predators will soon totally reject the child, making excuses as not to see them. The predator does their best to put a guilt trip on the victim, and any and all blame will be on the child. Plus any other scare tactics could be used—so the child will not tell, and the child is led to believe that all of this happened because they like it or wanted all of this to happen.

Stage III
Aftermath
False Remorse

Depending on the victim's response, the predator will be doing their best to make all the things that happened seem normal, was out of love for the child, and it is okay for two people to show their love for each other like *they* just did. What *they* just done was nothing like they hear on TV, or what their parent(s) and teachers say is bad. Of course, all are lies only to control the child and not for the child to tell. Truly, the predator doesn't care for the child at all; they want what they want when they want it; no true thoughts or feelings for the child at all. More likely than not, the predator will treat the child as an equal, as an adult. They will give the child attention, what the predator sees as love and affection. The child that is hungry for attention will begin to want to believe all the predator's lies. The victim maybe be lavished with gifts, money, whatever they were promised, so the victim will not tell. Which most of these gifts and money will be kept away from all questioning eyes of other family members.

Once this assault is over, the predator will do all they can to justify to the victim that what happened was completely all right. Even though the child will feel different.

Most predators will treat the child like royalty, giving the child whatever was promised to them and reassuring them there would be more gifts in the future.

The child will be totally dazed and confused of what had just happened. All along the predator will be praising the victim on how special that they are, how much they are cared for, and to never tell of ***their*** special secret games. That if they would ever tell no more gifts or money.

On the other hand, if the victim refuses the predator, most predators will apologize to the victim. Promise the victim that none of these things will *ever* happen again and not to tell anyone about *their* secret. If the victim gets scared and wants things to stop, the predator will do their best to reassure the child that nothing is wrong and relax. If that doesn't work and the victim still resists or wants all to stop, the predator will get scared the child will tell; most predators will stop the assault, then begin to apologize for scaring the victim and assure that these things will never happen again. So there is no need to tell of *our* secret games. The child, being petrified with fear, will agree not to tell, just so this horror will stop and for them to get to safety.

Everything the predator says to the child is trying to get the child to calm down, that they (the predator) didn't do anything wrong. Most predators will begin their "Blame Game." That the games *they* played is done by everyone that cares for or even loves each other like they do. Now *they* have a special secret that is never to be told to anyone. That all the things *they* did—there was nothing wrong in doing them, that the child is a grown-up now, and grown-ups do these special things all the time.

Of course, all are lies that are told by the predator to try to get the victim to accept what happened to them and that they nor the predator have done nothing wrong.

Sorry to say, the child will give in to the predator and try their best to hide their shame and pain. The abuse will continue until the predator gets tired of the victim or the child grows out of the predator's preference dynamics; or the predator finds another victim, or the predator gets caught. Sad, but very true, most all predators have a particular victim type in mind, the child's age range, hair and eye color, all the way to the child's body shape and size. This is called an "ideal victim type." Most predators will hunt, stalk, and search for different victims that may fit their liking, before they even make first contact.

All of this is very true about most predators; then when the child grows older, grows out of the predator's ideal victim rang, the predator will search for another child to replace the first one (if they haven't done this already), so on and so on until the predator is finally caught.

All the child ever wanted is appropriate love and attention from their family, along with kindness, understanding, and acceptance. Sadly, this precious child, this victim, will live in this hell and torment forever—for the rest of their life.

Other predators could be more aggressive, to scare the child not to tell. If this rejection is the case, the predator will soon stop going around the child, only checking in from time to time to see if the child has changed their minds. (If the predator comes around at all.) The predator could not care less about the victims or their families left in their wake. The victims are left with these horrendous nightmares that could devastate their entire lives forever, for as long as they live.

How could any human being ever want to devastate a child's life like that?

As loose as most morals are in the society today, one would think that one could find a consenting, age-appropriate **adult** to be with instead of harming a child. There is no rhyme nor reason for any of this destruction; it's a reality. These things do happen. These issues need to be more aggressively addressed, with knowledge and options to confronting these problems. Not repeatedly shoved into the deep, dark crevices of society's closets. ("Out of Sight, Out of Mind" has never worked; it just allows the monster to grow even worse.) Becoming more aware of early warning signs in the child's behavior, their attitudes, how they treat themselves, their siblings, their friends.

Above all else, your child needs to know that they are loved, that they can come to you at **any time** to talk to you about **anything**, and that you will truly, lovingly help them all you can.

Trying To Find Normalcy

Most predators know what they are doing is wrong. Some have taken years to justify and to rationalize—to themselves—that what they are doing is okay and that they are not hurting anyone. Some predators even try to find some normalcy in a heterosexual life style, only to convince themselves that this type of life is not for them. They have convinced themselves they have failed miserably and soon go back to old behaviors.

I would like to share the following with you all.

First Girlfriend. One of the guys that I was hanging around with at the time asked me how old I was (at that time.) "Twenty-two. Why?" I asked.

"Don't you have a girlfriend or a wife?" one of the guys asked.

"No." I chuckled. "I have not found a woman that would put up with me yet." Then the guys went on and on about this one girl that they know who reminded them a lot like me, but she was a girl.

"So, do you want to check out this chick, man?" one of the guys asked.

"Maybe sometime. I just don't need women problems right now," I said.

"Some of us were thinking that you may be gay, since you don't have a girlfriend and you want to hang out with guys like us," one of the guys mentioned. Needless to say that I got upset.

"Who said that I'm gay? Just because I hang out with you guys and enjoy being with you guys don't mean that I'm a faggot. Man," I said as I stopped the car, turned around, and headed back to town.

"Dude, none of us said that. Some of the other guys said that. Then my mom told me to watch out for you that you don't try anything."

Another one of the guys said, "Look."

I stopped the car right where I was still in the country. "If one of you think that I'm gay, get out right now, RIGHT NOW! I'm not going to worry about one of you thinking that I'm going to hurt you. Man, just because I'm nice to you guys don't mean diddly, you hear me."

"Just sayin'," one of the guys tried to say.

"Well, say it to the streets as you walk your —happy a— into town."

"Okay, man, chill out. I know that you're cool, that you're okay." Then all of the guys began to agree.

"Okay, now if any of you guys have a problem with me, no one is forcing you to come, no one is forcing you to get into this car, right?" I told them.

"Okay, let's all have a couple of beers and jam on some tunes," I said, and all the guys agreed to that.

To that day they had never seen me that upset or angry; I was always mellow, happy, joyful, and jolly around them. I exploded, and this had to have caught them off guard.

Besides, the one guy that was doing most of the questioning, didn't party much after that day—that was cool too with me.

I was wanting to have a girlfriend. Maybe if I had a lady, a lady that was a lot like me, who would love me and care for me for me, not a ton of expectations of me, I may be able to get my life on track.

Be careful what you wish for—this wish was quickly answered to my surprise, with a lady who was more like me than I could ever imagine.

One evening, I had a bunch of the guys with me, and we were drinking pretty good. Soon, I would take them out to the country, where we would stay the night, sleep off our drinks before I took them home. While we were riding, around one of the guys saw this car. "There she is. Right there. The girl we were telling you about," one of the guys said.

"Who? Which girl?" I said excitedly,

"Sara, the girl we said that reminded us of you," one of the guys said. "Yeah, I see her too. Honk your horn, flash your lights," another one of the guys said.

I did, and she soon pulled over in this old Chevy, in mint condition. A couple of the guys then jumped out of my car and ran to the car where this lady was waiting.

Then the guys that got out of the car to talk to her began to wave me to come up and talk to her.

I did go up to her car. She wasn't a knock-out fox, but she had a beautiful smile, and a pleasant attitude to go with it. We introduced ourselves, then she said: "Finally I get to meet you. That's all these guys talk about at times is you. Here you are in real life."

"Yeah, I get the same on this end as well," I said with a nervous smile.

"Look, I have parties out at my place all the time. These guys know when I will have one. Load them up and come out to have some fun," Sara explains.

"Sounds cool to me," I said.

"Good, let's say next Friday night," she said.

"I have to work next Friday," I said quickly.

"Cool, a man that has a job, that's good," Sara says with a smile, jokingly. "What time do you get off of work?" asked Sara.

"About eleven or twelve midnight," I said.

"Cool, bring some beer if you can afford it, bring a few of these guys, they all know where I live and I'll see you next Friday night." Sara said confidently.

"Sounds good, I'll be there," I said.

Trust me, the guys were far more excited about all of this than I was at the time. I did have a great time at her party that night; I actually enjoyed myself.

When Sara and I noticed that we were having feelings for each other, she told me something that rocked my world. Sara told me that she was a nymphomaniac.

Then I dropped my bomb on her:

"Sara, I'm old fashioned on this one thing. I truly believe in NO sex before marriage," I said, as her mouth dropped open and she looked at me like I'm crazy. "Look, I am beginning to really like you, I want to respect you and keep you for that special day. This is really the only rule that I have really."

"Wow, I didn't think that there was any of you guys left," Sara said.

"All I know there is one of us, and that is me." She didn't want to accept that, but she did; this didn't stop her from trying to get me, but I stood fast to this rule—with her. (We went together for almost a year before I broke up with her. I was getting weaker and weaker as for having sex. I cannot have sex with her; if she got pregnant, Mom would kill me. These were some of the old tapes, I told myself, and I wanted to believe at that time.)

Later, I found out that Sara was more like me than I thought she was all along. I found her with one of the very guys that party with me a lot. You know, I remembered how upset I was at him for being with my woman. I was very upset at her for being with one of my close friends; this was very upsetting and confusing to me. This just turned me against women even more; I wanted nothing to do with women for some time after that.

Second Girlfriend

I had this ongoing inner battle within myself to stop hurting others and focus on a happy life of heterosexuality, like most other people.

Sometime later, I was working in another city at this nice restaurant, and I met the other lady. She was beautiful to me. She was about my age, twenty-four or twenty-five years old, great sense of humor. I thought that she was beautiful inside and out. Surprisingly, I was beginning to have feelings for her. I really liked her, and I was even a little excited when I sat by her. I was thinking, just thinking at one time this may be the lady for me. She seemed to care for me as well. I soon found out that she was still married and in the middle of a divorce, but she was not divorced at this time. I told her that there is no way that I am going to "play in someone's back yard" when she was still married. I wouldn't want this to happen to me, and I would not do anything like that to anyone else. (Another old-fashioned belief of mine at the time, just an excuse.) I also told Mandy that I believe in No Sex before marriage; she looked at me strangely: "Sorry, I will not wait that long," Mandy said seriously. "Look, I will be divorcing my husband, for you. I agreed that there would be no closeness until after the divorce. That became final the other day. I'm here with you and that is where I want to be. I will not or cannot wait until we decide to get married, if we ever do decide on this." We talked about this again and again; I had this fear of having sex with a woman. I had all the old garbage that I remembered from Mom. I carried all the garbage my mom and peers told me of my size and how I would never make a woman happy. Topped all that with my own thoughts, fears, and beliefs, along with I have *never* had sex with a woman before; Mandy would be my first lady. I prayed and prayed about this like one would never believe. This was one of those rare times that I truly wanted to prove to myself that I am a man, that I can make a woman happy and satisfy her. I wanted this to work so badly; then maybe I could live a normal life with this lady that I was beginning to love. I believed it got to the point I had to do something. I had to man up or I was going to lose her. She has been so patient all this time, and she wanted to be with me on a much deeper level. One day I got brave enough to make plans for Mandy to stay overnight with me. I knew she had a very young son. I did not know that she was going to bring him along, but then again, I didn't tell her not too either.

After getting her son to asleep, we lay in bed next to each other, talked for a while. Then things began to heat up. I was getting excited and hyped to have some awesome fun. I had myself all psyched up; I wanted to do all that I can, not only for her, but also for me as well. I wanted so much to make her happy. I wanted to be happy, because she was happy. Then reality came crashing down, as seconds later I was lying next to her side smoking a cigarette. Mandy had to be lying there wondering when I was going to start, why a break already. I was so humiliated. I was telling myself just how much of a loser that I was. I was playing all of those tapes in my head of what my peers have said to me. I had thoughts of my mom and my peers looking at me, pointing down at me and laughing at me.I cried. Mandy soon put her hand on my arm and said: "This happens sometimes, don't beat yourself up," to comfort me. It helped a little, but I wanted so much for things to work out. She tried to get things restarted, but I just could not get things together. This was to be her night and my night; I had so much I wanted to prove to her, and myself especially. I failed miserably. I failed the both of us.

The next weekend I invited Mandy to stay again. This time she came alone, which was a good thing. Again, the same thing happened. I was totally finished in seconds. Mandy didn't say a word. She just tuned over with her back toward me, as I lit up my cigarette and tried to chill out. I did not think that I could ever be more embarrassed, more humiliated and upset at myself than the other day when I failed—again it was that night. I told myself then, "That's it! Never again." I had myself convinced that night. This would be the last time that I ever face this degree of humiliation again. I have been told that this happens all of the time; most men work through those issues and go on with an excellent, healthy relationship. I did not want to, nor did I let myself work through those issues.

That was Mandy's last night with me; she soon moved onto a man this time.

Third Girlfriend

I was back living in this one city again; I was an assistant manager at another restaurant at the time. This one waitress started this day, and for some reason, she was attracted to me. I don't know if it was me she was attracted to or the position that I had at that time. Soon, we became friends, and we began to have feelings for each other. She was wanting much more than this, and I then told her about my belief in having "No Sex Before Marriage"; this did not go over with her at all. She laughed. "You have got to be kidding me?" As she began to shuffle my hair around.

"What, what are you doing?" I asked.

"I don't see a halo up there. I think I see a couple of horns. I know you have one somewhere," Caren said as she laughed. After she saw that I was serious: "I never thought that I would meet a saint," Caren said in a serious voice. "I'm not a saint nor devil; this is just one of my beliefs. I will respect the lady, then, when we get married, then have all the fun that we want, then," I explained.

Soon I found out that Caren was still married as well. I was upset about this as to why she didn't tell me. "Does it really matter?" Caren asked.

"YES, TO me it does. I don't want anyone playing in my back yard, and I will not play in anyone else's," I said. "Why are you trying to hex this relationship before things even get started? When and if you get a divorce from your husband, then we get to talk about sharing our lives together, not until you are divorced," I said. Caren did not say too much about this at all. She never talked about if the divorce has been filed or even began yet. She came to work from time to time saying that her husband beat her and their daughter. That she hated him and could not wait to get away from all of that hell. One night she called me at work and asked if I would pick her up; her husband was drunk, beat the crap out of her, and she wanted to leave. After I was finished at work, I went to pick her up. She thought that I was going to take her home with me, but I didn't. Her daughter was safe at her parents' house, and she just had to get away from that hellhole. She was telling me when her husband gets drunk or high how he beats her, cusses her out. This time he was drunk and tore up the house. She was crying on and off, saying how all of this hell was coming to an end soon.

I then pulled into this one motel downtown, and Caren asked: "Why are we here?"

"This is where you will be staying the night."

"But...I thought I was going to your place?" Caren replied.

"Caren, I said no sex before marriage, and this is what I mean. I will get you a room for the night, and in the morning I will come back and I will take you to breakfast, then take you to your parents with your daughter," I said.

"I want you to stay with me—why won't you stay with me?" Caren begged. I got her a room. I went up to the room with her. She had done her best to try to get me to stay, and I refused. "I'll see you in the morning," I said as I kissed her on the cheek, and then I left.

The next morning, I went back to get her for breakfast. Caren was gone. I checked with the clerk at the desk. "I don't think she was here five minutes after you left. She came right through here and left."

I was angry. I wasted all that money for nothing. I was trying to help her, and she left. I did have her mom and dad's telephone number, and I called them up to see if she was there. They told me she wasn't there and that they still had her daughter.

Later I found out that Caren's parents had her daughter quite frequently.

I did not know where she could possibly be. I went home to soon get ready for work, and I knew that Caren worked or was supposed to work that night I may see her then. When I saw her at work, I could tell that she was in no condition to work. I first asked her where she went.

"Caren, I went back to the motel to pick you up this morning. You weren't there. Where did you go?"

"I went home," Caren said. "Can't you tell?" Caren had a few black and blue bruises on her arms and a black eye.

"Why?" I asked seriously, lovingly.

"I wasn't going to stay in that motel all by myself. I was going to sleep on the streets, like I have done before. Instead, I hitchhiked my way back home, and he was there; it was a knock out, drag out most of the morning."

"You know that you can't work like this—" I tried to say.

"Then what am I going to do? I have no money, I have no place to stay," Caren said frantically.

"Caren, go home with your child. Your mom, dad and your child need you, and you need them," I tried to explain to her.

"Yeah —right," Caren said as she went to the phone to call someone to pick her up. We started to get busy at work, and I wasn't able to see who finally picked Caren up, if anyone.

Caren called me at work a few times to keep up to date on how she was doing. I called her parents to check up on her, and most of the time they hadn't seen her, but they still had her daughter. I didn't know the whole story there, why Caren felt that she could not go home. At first I had no idea. Later I found out a lot of facts about her and her family. When Caren came back to work, she appeared to be all happy and joyful. She walked up to me and said: "It's done, it's final!"

"What...what is?" I asked.

"I'm a free woman at last," Caren said.

"All right!" I said as I gave her a kiss and a big hug. "Fantastic. No one needs to live in that crap. I'm glad that you are finally out of there," I said. Caren was telling me all about it, and I was getting just as excited as she was about this. I knew the hell and the torment that I went through as a child. I just imagined that she was going through the same thing, if not a lot worse.

Mental and physical abuse can be very devastating to anyone, and no one needs to live through any of that abuse. Later that evening, she asked me when could she move in with me.

"Caren, no, we can't do that right now," I said.

"I thought that when the divorce was final that we could—"

"Caren, I have been very upfront with you, and you should have known that this would not happen," I tried to explain.

Caren gave me a serious look and said: "We'll talk later." As she stormed off to wait on her customers.

One of the employees that I was friends with smiled and continued to work at his fryers. "Don't say a word," I told him jokingly.

One day when I got to work, my boss said that he needed to talk to me about something. We sat down and he gave me the news. "The owners are needing an assistant manager to go to their store in another state to help out one of the owners' sons manage that store. They asked me if I had anyone that I could send. I mentioned you. Now you don't have to accept, you are doing very good right here. I would hate to lose you," my manager explained. "This is a little more pay, and all of your expenses will be paid to move. I told them that I would let you know about this, see what you say, then let them know your decision."

"Wow. I have never been to that state or city before," I said.

"I have traveled through it. It's not bad; it's a nice college town. When the fall semester begins that city doubles in population," my manager explained.

"That sounds exciting." I said, a little speechless at the time.

"Well, take a couple of days. I told them I would call them back on Monday with your answer," my manager said.

"Thank you, sir, for this chance. I will let you know. I will think about this some more," I said, and then I went to work. I was all excited about this potential job promotion; I couldn't wait to tell Craig and Terry, a couple of my friends. They would be really excited about it too.

When I told them, they didn't seem to be too excited, but then Terry asked: "That's a long way from here. How will we ever see you?"

Craig echoed the same thing.

"I don't know. I'm sure that I will be back from time to time. Most all of my friends are here," I tried to reassure them.

"Does Caren know about this yet?" asked Craig.

"No, when I see her, I will tell her," I replied.

Man, I thought that they would really be excited for me, but they appeared to be more worried about them not seeing me again. (All I was thinking about at this time was myself, how happy that I would be about this promotion. I was not thinking about the guys and how they would miss me or any of their feelings about this transfer.) (Also, I hadn't thought of Caren's thoughts and feelings about this either. When I did, I kind of felt good, because I felt that I was getting away from her.)

I had mixed emotions about this whole thing, really; I didn't really want to leave my friends because we were all pretty close. Then things were getting too close with Caren and I, and this would get me away from her to think things out a little more, before I made any commitment to her about us marrying. When I told Caren about this, at first she was really happy, than when she found out that she was not going with me; that she didn't like at all. She began to cry and ask me why she could not go along. I tried to explain that I wasn't ready (I was in my late twenties I believe). I needed more time to think about things. This was something that Caren did not want to hear. Caren tried her best to convince me to let her go along. I said no. That if she would hold up for a couple of weeks, let me get settled in, I would come and get her and then she would spend some time with me.

She did not want to hear that line either. She saw that Craig was going with me, why not her. Craig was coming to help me move into my new place, then Terry was going to come a couple of weeks later to stay with me for a while.

Well, I soon got all of my things in my tag-along trailer, and Craig and I headed for my new home.

A couple of weeks later, a couple of other friends were with me, Terry and Lois, and stayed with for a while.

This one evening I get a call—from Caren, while I was still at work. She had run off with a carnival and now was somewhere up north of us. After work, I picked up Terry and Lois and we went hunting Caren down. When we found her, she did not look healthy at all. We all got back to my place where she cleaned up, and we ate. I asked her what she was thinking when she ran off from her family to join that carnival. Did we all get a story and a half. Mainly, she said: "I wanted to be here with you," Caren said with tears in her eyes. We sat and talked for a while, and then we got ready to go to bed.

On my day off, I loaded everyone up and took them back home. I took Caren to her mom and dad's, where they all talked me into staying the night. I told Caren I wanted to get settled in. I wanted to be on the job for a while before she came to live with me. I was just not ready right now. She seemed to understand, but knowing Caren, it was hard to tell.

That night, I let my guard down. I was intimate with Caren. Again, I was so upset with myself. I was so embarrassed and humiliated with myself. In seconds, for me, it was over; this was the last time that I attempted to have sex with a woman. If I ever had a dream, an inkling to have a normal heterosexual relationship, that ended that night, that's it. It had nothing to do with Caren. None of this was her fault. I could not perform, and I did not have enough to satisfy her nor me. I wanted to just leave right then and there, but I didn't. I waited until morning.

There was a part of me that really wanted this to work; I wanted to prove to myself and to Caren that I could do this. I wanted to be able to make Caren happy and want to be with me for ALL that I could be, not just for my personality. (With all of my issues, I would never let a relationship with a woman work; I was demanding too much from myself. I had my sights set too high. I wanted to be a friend, lover, and a couple that would spend forty, fifty years happily married together, both of us making this choice together.)

My Son?!

It was five years later I was back working in the same city I was before my transfer. I was working for another restaurant for a little over a year, and I was doing pretty well. I was doing really well in management that they transferred me over to one of their busier stores within the city. One day when I came to work, there was Caren. I had not seen her in over five years, and I couldn't believe it. Later, we got talking. I found out that she got married again and divorced, had another child, and he was about five years old. She was still having problems but was getting by. She was trying to get on her feet after the divorce (just like the last time we met) with her life still "helter-skelter" it sounded like. She asked me if I found anyone yet. I said: "Still haven't found anyone to put up with me yet." She was letting me know that she wanted to get back with me again. We talked and talked from time to time. She gave me her number and her parents' telephone number; I then gave her my telephone number (reluctantly).

A few days later, she sprung a huge surprise on me. She brought an eight-by-ten picture of her son into work to show me.

"This is my son. What do you think?"

"He is a very handsome young man," I replied with a smile.

"Yeah, he is something else," Caren said.

"How old is he?" I asked her.

"He will soon be five in January," Caren replied.

"You must be proud of him," I said, looking at the picture, wishing he was also my child.

Then Caren asked with a kind of pride in her voice: "Does he look like anyone that you may know?"

I looked closely at the child in the picture; I kind of thought that he may look a little like me, but no way. "No, not really. Why?"

Caren than looked disgusted, a little upset, and said: "Come on, take a closer look. He's your son, he is our son."

At first, I didn't hear her right; I didn't hear what I really wanted to hear. "Who did you say, Caren?" I questioned, to make sure that I heard correctly.

"Bryon is your son!" Caren repeated, point blank. I was really floored. I was speechless at first, and I had a million and one emotions racing through my mind. I was extremely happy, happy that I had a son in my life. I was able to do something right in my life. That one night wasn't totally wasted. (The way that I thought it was at that time.)

I couldn't believe it, but I wanted to believe it so much. I began to get very emotional. I asked Caren: "Why didn't you contact me? Tou had my telephone number where you could have called my family. You could have left a message to tell me that you were with my child, and I would have been here for you. I would have been through his whole birth with you. You know me, you know that I would not have left you like that," I said through my tears.

"I wanted you to be with me for me, and not because I was with your child," Caren explained.

"I'm a father for almost five years and not know it…. How could…" I left the office where we were talking and went to the walk-in. I broke down and I was crying profusely. I was shaken with sadness, hurt, and pain and shame, that I have thrown so much of my life away. I was a dad and didn't know it. My heart was deeply torn of this news. (My childhood without my father was racing through my mind.) I was in this walk-in, at work; I was trying to compose myself to get ready for the supper rush.

Caren came into the walk-in with me and asked: "What's wrong with you? I thought that you would be happy with this news."

"I am happy, Caren. It's that I have lost five years with you and our son. This makes me sad, sad that I didn't chose to stay with you instead of taking off." I was trying to explain through my tears and broken heart. Caren saw my pain and tried to comfort me; I had to get ready for supper. It was by the very strength of God that I was able to compose myself enough to do just that. Caren gave me the picture of Bryon and told me that I could have it. When I got home, I put it on this shelf in the front room. I was so proud of that little guy, and I had not even met him yet.

I was doing pretty good at the place where I was working. I had a small apartment, and I was wanting to get a bigger place for when Caren and both of the children to move in with me. (Sara was about twelve years old at the time, and Bryon was going on five years old.) So I began to search the papers for a trailer or house, something larger than what I have at this time. To make a very long story short, I found out through my search that Ron and Mary (Caren's parents) had their old trailer for sale. I didn't know this. At first, I was going through the realtor for the place. I was looking for a contract for deed set up, and the realtor said that the family would not go for that. I did get a telephone number, so I soon got the nerve to call the family to talk to them.

This is when I soon found out that this was Caren's mom and dad that was selling their old place. They had no problem of selling it to me on a contract for deed, but they needed so much down to pay some of their expenses on the place; I could not swing that money. What was awesome was I was able to begin my friendship with them once again, to Caren's surprise. I kind of felt after I told Caren that I talked to her dad and I was trying to buy their old trailer, she seemed very surprised, even shocked. I explained all of this to her about wanting to get a bigger place and all for her and the kids. I thought that she would be happy, but she was kind of distant, acting a little strange. "What's wrong, Caren? I thought that you would be excited about all of this?" I said.

"I am—it's just a little quick. That's what has caught me off guard," Caren said, like in a very uncertain voice.

"So when will I get to see Byron and Sara?" I would like to get to know them a bit before the move," I replied.

"Now, let's not move so quickly. We just can't move in and me tell Byron that you're his dad. He still thinks that my ex-husband is his dad. Things like this have to be handled carefully," Caren explains nervously.

"Okay, I understand that. I agree. I would like to meet them and let's go from there," I said.

"Let me talk this over with Mom and Dad first. Let me see what they think is the best thing to do for now," Caren says nervously.

"Sounds good to me. So when will you do this?" I asked.

"Soon, soon, give me just a little time, okay?" Caren said as she walked off, in disgust because of my pressing. There I stand, kind of puzzled, with a million and one more questions going through my head. I was all hyped, excited, and pumped about being a father. Me—ME having a son—me, a son—ME a dad..? Wow!

Later, Caren told me not to say anything to her parents about me being Bryon's dad; she told me that she would take care of that. "They don't know the truth either?" I asked.

"No, I have my reasons. Just hang tight, okay?" Caren said. "It's been over five years and now you want everything to change overnight. Something this delicate as a child's life had to be taken in small steps." I couldn't believe what I just heard from Caren.

A brief period of time went on here. Caren and I was getting closer (I thought), and we seemed to be getting along pretty good.

I was staying focused on my job, thinking about the future with Caren and the kids. I was really on "Cloud 9"; this was the closest that I have ever felt how it was to be a father, to begin to feel—well, normal.

I was thanking and praying to God for this blessed news and a chance to be a father to one of His choice children.

I couldn't wait to spread the good news; I could not wait to have Bryon in my arms for the first time, to hold MY son.

At that point in time, I had been kept away from Ron and Mary for some reason. Caren kept coming up with reasons that her parents didn't want to see me, that they were upset with me for not buying their trailer or something like that. I felt that something was not right. I wanted to see my son. I wanted to begin a relationship with him and his sister; now Caren is throwing up all of these smoke screens for some reason.

At this point I felt that I had waited long enough. I called Ron one day and asked if I could come by to talk for a few minutes on my way to work. Ron seemed to be excited about my call and wanted to see me too. Ron gave me their address, and I stopped by briefly.

Here I met Bryon for the first time. I almost broke down right in front of Ron and Bryon. Ron was a big man, and little Bryon was clinging on to his grandpa's pant leg, hiding behind Ron and peeking around to see me talking to his grandpa, with a little smile on his face. (This reminded me of myself and Mom on my first day of school.) "He's a little bashful, if you can tell," Ron said.

"Yeah, I could tell," I replied. Ron and I talked for a few minutes. Ron invited me back anytime to visit. Sara wanted to meet me too, but I had to get going to work.

When I told Caren that I stopped by to talk to her dad, she got all upset. "I hope that you didn't say anything about Bryon?" she snapped at me.

I looked very puzzled as I said: "No, I didn't say a word about Bryon. I saw him, though; he was hanging onto his grandpa's pant leg," I explained with a smile.

"Him and his grandpa are really close. That's really the only male that Bryon really knows," Caren said sadly.

"That will soon change," I said.

"Let me break this news about Bryon now," Caren said.

"Yeah, yeah, I just want to get things moving. I have so much to get caught up on," I said as I walked close to Caren to kiss her.

"Just let me handle Bryon," Caren said as she pecked me on the cheek and went to work.

Soon, weeks went by, and Caren always had excuses to tell me about how it's not time yet, she doesn't want to tell him, and I go running off again; she had a thousand and one excuses.

I was at Ron and Sara's one evening. Both kids were in bed, and it was just us three there. I finally got the nerve to ask them about Bryon. "Caren told me the other day that Bryon was my son. I'm wanting to believe that he is. He looks like me, and I feel a bonding there—I don't know?"

"Is that what Caren told you?" Mary asked me.

"Yes, that is what she told me when I saw her for the first time," I said.

"You know you can't hardly believe anything she says," Ron said.

"If anyone knows I guess it would be her," Mary said in a very questionable voice.

"When she told me, I was really happy, and then distraught because I wasn't here to help her go through all of this," I explained.

"When did all of this supposedly happen?" Ron asked.

"The last night that I stayed with you all before going back to Glowington. That was just a little over five years ago," I said.

"Did you know that she was still married to Bryon's father at that time?" Ron said with a little smile on his face.

"She swore to me that she had been divorced at that time," I said surprisingly.

"You can't believe half of what she says. She lies all of the time," Mary (her mother) said.

"I bet she hasn't told you that we had to adopt her kids or we would have lost them to the state?" Ron (her father) said with a smirk.

"No, she said that you guys were watching her kids while she works," I said. I was stunned to find out these things. How could anyone lie about something as precious as their children?

"So, what did you have in mind? What are you wanting to do?" Mary asked.

"I was thinking about when Caren and I get married, I was going to adopt Bryon and his sister Sara. I really want to be their father to take care of them and to love them," I explained.

"Since I highly respect both of you, that is why I needed to talk these things over with you guys, and I'm glad I did too," I said.

Needless to say when I saw, Caren I brought all of this to her, and I wasn't a "happy camper." I cannot and will not share all of the things that I said from this broken heart that has been lied to once again by "a woman."

I asked her why she lied about her divorce many years ago when we briefly went together. Why she told me that her parents were just watching the kids, when they rescued her children from the state and they adopted both of them? Why she said this. Why she did that. Then I said what was really tearing me up at that time. I looked deep into Caren's eyes, and I said with tears in my eyes: "As much as I would truly love for Bryon to be my son, I am beginning to doubt that he is. I can't believe you, Caren."

Caren said little to her defense this whole time, but she did say: "I should know who the father of my son really is."

"I believe that, but are you telling me that I am Bryon's father or 'today' I am the one *you* want to be Bryon's father? That is my question?"

"Believe what you want to. You are Bryon's father," Caren said as she began to walk away.

"I want to believe you, but only if it is the truth!" I insisted.

A few days later, I received the straw that broke the camel's back; I was with Ron and Mary, and they asked me: "Bryon has a rare blood disorder. Do you have any rare blood conditions?"

"No, I have nothing like that," I said.

"This blood disorder is hereditary that he would have received from his father. His dad has that rare blood disorder—you don't," Mary said. I broke down again, right there, right there in front of them. They did their best to console me—with little luck. I was so angry at Caren I could verbally tear her apart. My heart was devastated once again by a woman. All of the old issues and old tapes I was blaring in my head. This was the utmost final straw, and I was never intimate with another woman again. I would talk to women, but I kept all of them at arm's length, far away from my broken heart.

That was it with Caren. After I calmed down the best that I could, I told her that I wanted her as far away from me as possible and that I never wanted to see her again.

She ended up going with my roommate at the time; she ended up in my house anyway.

As for the beautiful picture that Caren gave me, her mother came to visit me one day. Her mother saw the picture sitting on the mantel with other pictures. "That's mine," Mary exclaimed. "I wondered where it went to. Caren, why did you take that picture?" Mary said with tears in her voice.

"It's my kid, my picture. I gave it to you," Caren said jokingly.

"You gave it to me, though," her mom said, as she picked up the picture lovingly and looked at it.

"Mary, it's yours take it with you," I said.

"No, she gave it to you now; it's yours," Mary said sadly, as she put it back on the mantel. Before she left, I handed her the picture. She accepted it and gave me a kiss on the cheek before she left.

I told myself, "That's it. I can't let this guard down again to a woman—ever."

How broken, confused, and devastated this child had to be, how all alone he had to feel. Massive trust issues, the anger and rage that fester inside of him to this day.

My focus quickly went to "Me, Me." My heart, spirit, soul, and my will I let to be broken by different women in my life.

Through all these years I wanted so much to be loved, accepted, cared for just for me, and just to be "normal"—whatever that was—I didn't even know that... I truly wanted the "normal" American Dream, grow up, have a nice job, a wife, a family, two children, a cat, dog, a home with lots and lots of love. This was a dream in America; it was not my American Dream.

I cannot remember all of the countless times that I have fallen to my knees and prayed, prayed and begged God for His help. I felt that I never received it (at those times in the past). I let this monster have total control of my being. I felt that this want, this compulsive behavior that I had. This thing had control over me; it possessed me; I had no control over it. (I know now that I did have the power; this was an excuse to continue to do what I wanted to do all along.)

Another very depressing fact is, before the predator is caught, the first time—within the court system—chances are very high that the predator has had many victims before this time. The predator has lied, begged, maybe even bought the silence of many victims and their families, before this first time in court; very sad but very true. Some of the predators have run from city to city, state to state, even country to country, doing their best to evade detection and arrest.

Once I worked through my "poor me," "everyone hates me," I began to seriously want to find out the answers to my questions of when, where, why and how come I chose to do all the things that I did—for so long. A number of times I wanted to have a normal heterosexual life during these past years. I didn't know how. I really just didn't want to was the main reason.

I began my journey into a deep self-introspection. Why was I so obsessed with this erratic behavior? "Why me? Why me?" echoed through the foundations of my being.

After many hours of therapy, I was slowly beginning to find some answers to these nagging questions of mine. Which produced more questions of "WHY" and searching deeper for these answers. The programs I were in, and the therapists I had were awesome, and they slowly helped me peel back the layers of a sick facade that I took years in building around myself. The years of justifications, sick rationalizations that I chose to believe in order for me to continue what I wanted to do.

One of the many things I began to realize was I was hurting, deeply. I hated myself, my family, everyone and almost everything around me. I felt that I was a total and complete failure, a loser, and everyone hated and despised me, including God Himself. I felt useless, worthless around family, and soon peers, and I sought some solace where it seemed I had the most control.

One of the many things I was asked to do, in therapy, was to write my autobiography (a detailed account of my childhood, teens, on into adulthood) the best that I could remember.) Write about the good times and bad times. Detailing some of my thoughts, feelings, and how I chose to behave in those times. So I could begin to see the making of this monster. I was not born this "monster"; I was not born to hurt and to destroy other people's lives. I was blaming everyone else for my shortcomings, the cause of all my anger, hatred, and vengeful behavior.

I felt that life hated me, and I needed to protect myself at all costs, and it seemed that I found some refuge within my distorted behavior, no matter how brief this relief might have been.

One of the main things I was learning was "Victim Empathy."

Stage IV
FORGIVENESS!!!

BEGINNING...SELF

"Judge not, and you shall not be judged. Condemn not, and you shall not be condemned. Forgive, and you shall be forgiven. Luke 6:37 *(NKJV)*

An Epiphany

One day, while in the county jail, a pastor stopped by to talk to some of the prisoners. One finally got up the nerve to confess his suicidal thoughts and some of the reasons why. He also confessed to some of the other things he has done and how he felt that even God hated him and God was sending him into eternal damnation—for life. The pastor touched the man's shaking hand and said very seriously: "Son, God does not hate you. God does not like the life you choose. He loves you. He loves you so much that you are finally here to get the help and direction. You have said you have prayed for—for so long. We need to rejoice, that your prayers have been answered..." A ray of Hope as his thoughts slowly began to change.

Most all of us have regrets in our lives. May it be for things we have said or done. Or for some things we never got around to say or do for someone.

Everybody, that is ANYBODY, is made up of "GOOD" and "Evil," "Good Parts and Bad Parts." We all have things that we LIKE about ourselves and things that we all don't like about ourselves. Still, all of these parts are us. ALL of these GOOD parts are in us, and ALL of the Bad parts are in us too. So we will need to learn to accept all of who we are, because these inner battles will hold us up going through our "Survivor Process."

Envision I:

On a more personal note, when you were a child, or even today, as an adult, how did you feel or how do you feel when you think that you are being rejected, unloved, not accepted? Some may try to get some type of attention, even if it is negative, wrong, or bad attention. Now, how do you feel when you are loved, accepted, and people embrace you for you? Now, please take a minute—let's think and feel how good this feels, how warm and encouraging this all feels. How awesome this feeling is to you. I am loved, I am accepted, people do love me, I am cared for. How good do you feel knowing and hearing this? I feel really awesome inside. This is how it will feel when we learn to embrace all of our selves totally, completely.

If we cannot feel comfortable and accept who we are, how can we ever begin to have anyone else love us? How we think about ourselves is projected in our thoughts, feelings, and behavior of our everyday lives.

Envision II:

Here is one more way that may help to get to the level of accepting all parts of ourselves: Most all of us have heard of "King Arthur and the Knights of the Round Table." The key part here is to envision King Arthur calling all of his knights to a meeting, and they are sitting around this huge, round table. Why a round table, one may ask? Because every knight was very special, very unique in their own right, but equal when sitting at this table. There was not one knight that was any more important than the next. They were all human beings with good and bad in them all; they all had equal power, equal voice in this circle, and they were all a part of this family of knights of this period in time. No one sat at the head of this table, for all were on an equal plain. (The king was the king, of course, but he chose this round table, so all could feel equally accepted and equally important.)

> In your mind, envision this beautiful, huge, round table in front of you. For now, for this moment there is only you sitting at this table; you just chose one of the many seats; all of the seats are all the same; not one seat is any more important or more comfortable than the other; they are all the same.

> Now think of all the "Good" parts of ourselves (our "sense of humor," "our kindness," "loving," etc.). Let them take a set at this table. Now you

don't seat them because all seats are the same and there is not one seat more important than the other. This is the reason for these parts to seat themselves.

> After all of these parts have been seated, now think of all the bad parts of you and ask "Them" to seat themselves. "WOW!" Now look around this huge table and begin to see all of these special parts of what make you—You. This is an awesome feeling ("AWESOME" is at this table as well; he's over there among Doubt and Disbelief.) Amazingly, in this picture, everyone is getting along, everyone is getting the attention, everyone is being acknowledged, everyone is feeling your love and acceptance. That is why there is so much harmony, peace, and warmth in this picture.

NOW, let one of these parts begin to feel rejected, not loved, and they will throw a fit until you accept them, embrace them, and bring them back to this round table where they feel your love for them.

This was our first huge step in our "Forgiveness Process" because we have to accept ourselves for ALL that we are. We have to learn to love all parts of us, all parts of us Good or Bad. Once we have done that, we need to "Forgive Ourselves," so we can soon forgive others.

This was kind of confusing to me. Now I'm being told to accept the very things that I—Now—hate in myself. (All of my anger, rage, resentment, etc.) This was the way that it was explained (metaphorically speaking), and it slowly began sinking in. When someone feels cared for, loved, accepted, and acknowledged, this person will be much more acceptable to change. When things that are pointed out to them that need to be changed, managed, controlled, this person is much more willing to change.

Now staying with the "round table" image—here are all of these different parts of you sitting at this table, good and bad. It makes no difference if you like or dislike any part of you; the fact is, all of these are parts of us good and bad—"accept" them, "embrace" them. You don't have to feed them or give them power of any kind any longer.

"Feeding Time!?"

Having to admit how deplorable that I was to even to myself was not easy at all. The more that I fought this, the more it raised its ugly head within me, and I allowed for this to steal my happiness in all of the other changes that I was making in my life. I have learned to accept these parts. I acknowledge this part of me, and I have learned to manage this part of me. "I don't have to dwell on this part. I don't feed it"—what does that mean? Like alcoholism, drug addiction, gambling, overeating to anorexia nervosa. All of these addictive behaviors can be managed, controlled, so one can live a healthier life, as long as we do not invest a lot of our time and our energy on any of them.

(One may have to seek professional help; if a crime has been committed do their time, seek help while doing this time.)

When you begin to want to go back to an old behavior, you need to stop all of those thoughts, get with a trusted friend that you can talk to, stop those thoughts, think of and do something else to get your mind off of this want, this desire, so you do not fall backwards and relapse into old behaviors.

Consider all of your hard work that you have achieved to that point, all of the changes and growth that you have made and all of the people that are very proud of you—then your sense of failure begins to haunt you.

<u>Caution:</u> Say that you have been close to a "High Risk" area for you— that day you had no problems, nor even urges. You may be able to do this many different times—may it be consciously or subconsciously. (May it be just one time or numerous times over days, months, or even years—you notice that you have not had one issue.) This is very dangerous for you! All it would take is one day that you would let your guard down, then your self-worth and self-esteem is in the pits; this is the beginning of you wanting to "Act Out" once again. (Also, a good time for you to "check yourself." What is going on in your life today? What has been troubling you?) If you don't take this "Time Out," you are "One Step Away" from PLUNGING yourself deep into old behaviors. (May it be going for just ONE drink with some friends or smoking just one "do-bee" with some friends you have not seen in ages.) Mostly, you must do all of this for you, you have to want—I said really want to make these changes in your life. It's when YOU truly want to make these changes is when you will do everything in your power to have a healthy life. (This can include smoking, if it is a bad habit that you have been trying to quit.)

What we are doing here is learning to like ourselves; yes, soon we can even LOVE ourselves. It's when we feel lower than a snake's belly or when we feel like the scum of the earth is when we do not care for no one and nothing, especially we do not care for ourselves. If we don't like ourselves; we may even hate ourselves, for whatever reason(s). No way we will respect nor love others. The word "Love" is so important here.

Do You Love Yourself? For most, the answer would be a resounding "Yes!"

"Do you really, truly LOVE yourself?" (I'm talking in a healthy way, not like a narcissist.) When I was asked this question, I was speechless at first, then I said: "No!" Mainly because of all the hell, devastation, and the torment that I was beginning to see in my life.

> I could not think of one accomplishment that I had ever made in my whole life, not one.

> Almost everything that I began or started I never finished. Either, I lost interest, I thought it was too hard, or there was really nothing in it for me. I had a very short attention span.

> I felt so hurt, abused, degraded, unloved, and all alone. I felt that I had no friends, no one cared for me, not even my close family. I really did feel alone even when I was in a room full of family or other people.

Now how could anyone in their right minds "LOVE" themselves?

Looking at the negative parts of yourself that you don't like, if you ignore them, pretend that these parts are not there, you even may try to forget it. This is called denial; this problem is still a part of you, and if you don't take care of these things, they will keep haunting you when you're least expected. So I had to acknowledge all of these parts of me that I didn't like. Over time, I began to embrace them. I began to learn to manage them (not to feed them), and I soon chose not to give them any power over me. (This is the beginning stages of learning about self-empowerment.)

People, this takes time. Our lives did not become a mess overnight, so one will have to repeatedly work on these areas of their life that they don't like and keep wanting to change them for the better—for themselves. Ways to do this are, you have a problem with drugs or alcohol, get involved in different classes/programs that will show you, help you, and encourage you in ways to stay clean and serene. If you have problems with anger, rage, developing relationships, one can read books on these issues to help them make the changes that is needed in their lives. Find and join a group(s). Same is true for any offenders: There are some very good therapists out there, right now. Truly seek and you will find all of the help that is needed for you.

Self-Empowerment

Also for you to learn how important self-empowerment really is for your new and changed development. We must know and fully understand that we are in complete control of ourselves, our lives, inside and out; we have this power; we are empowered, to change and manage ourselves. (We did not have control over all the things that happened to us, as children; TODAY, we are adults. We do have the power to change how we want these things to control and manipulate the rest of our lives is so vital in this process.) (Not for one second am I saying to forget the past. I'm not trying to lessen any of the hell that you have gone through, I'm saying we are adults now, we can't change one second of the past—it is NOW—this we do have control and power over to change—if you choose to, if you want too?)

NOW as adults—Learning that we NOW have total control over our thoughts, feelings, and our behaviors, also we have the power how we want our futures to become. Then to soon see that we have had this awesome power our whole adult lives—needs to empower us even more for us to take full control of our lives.

<u>Letting Go of Our Past</u>

The next thing is our past. We cannot change any of our pasts; there were many things that happened to us that were not our fault, but they happened to us anyway. There are many things that we have done or not done in our past; we cannot change any of that at all either.

If there is someone that you have wronged and you can make amends, *appropriately*, do so. If crime(s) have been committed and you have not taken responsibility for them, do so. In order to begin/continue your journey to forgive yourself, you must put these things on the table, all of your cards must be on the table, yes on your "Round Table" as well. You must be open and honest with <u>yourself</u>—if with no one else. See, you have to live with yourself;

you have to be with you twenty-four seven, so be true to you. I don't care what you have done. YOU know what you have done. YOU know "Right from Wrong." You may not want to see all of the hurt, pain, and anguish you have caused; you must acknowledge it, admit it to yourself so one can soon move on within their lives.

All of these are things in your past, things that have happened long ago, you cannot do one thing about any of these. Now is the time to stop giving all of those monsters, all of those ghosts—power over your life—let them go. You cannot change that past, but you do have total and complete control over everything now and in your future. Let's now focus on our future, the one thing that you can change and manage for yourself.

<u>Embracing The New You</u>

Knowing that you are a very special, very unique human being, there is not one other person exactly like you in this whole world, nor our universe. You have very special skills, special talents that are unique to only you. Then when you begin to see how special and unique that you really are, how valuable that you are, there will be these seeds of love that will be re-planted and watered within you. As this love for yourself grows—-and it will, if you let it—other people will begin to see these changes in you and your life will continue to blossom. Then you will begin to see this lovely person that you have been hiding all of these years—joyfully in front of you.

Loving and accepting yourself is an awesome thing; don't go to the extremes of bragging, boasting about yourself. Do not begin to think that you are better than anyone else, learn humility.

Yes, you are a very special person, then so is everyone; we are all special and unique in our own ways. You have now allowed yourself to join the "family," the human race.

Loving ourselves is so important. Because when we really care for and love ourselves, there will come a time when we will want to share this love with others. Since you have this joy of self in you, it is okay to share this with others.

To Forgive or Forgiveness

What does this mean?

> To give up resentment(s) of or claim to requital for an insult.
> To cease to feel resentment(s) against an offender;
> To grant relief from payment; to forget a debt(s) to you (Per Merriam Webster Dictionary)

Do you agree that we can be one of our own worst enemies? Some of us will even forgive others before we ever forgive ourselves. I know that I can and have in some cases. To continue our journey of forgiveness, it is imperative that we start with ourselves first. "But you have no idea all of the things that I have done wrong." True, if you have committed crime(s) that you haven't taken full responsibility for, do so.

Do your time, pay this debt to society for these things, for your sake, then make a commitment to yourself that when you are released you will have a clean slate for your new life. Seek help from professionals in the field of the issue(s) that you have; do not allow yourself to stay in the hell that you chose to keep yourself in one day longer.

<u>Spirituality</u>

Another thing that I did I began to seek God (or your Higher Power), once again.

I felt that God hated me; I thought that He despised me, and I was just a breath away from the Lord Himself destroying me and casting me into the lake of fire. Hell, internal damnation for eternity. I truly felt this way at that time. It took a while for me to work through these distorted beliefs that the devil tried to lay on my heart and tear at my very spirit. (Along with all of the mental tapes of my past I was holding on to.) God hates and despises all the horrific *things* that we have done, but God does not hate us. I am His child as well, and as long as I believe in Him, He will believe in me and LOVE me; He Loves me so much that God Himself was disciplining me.

(People, this thought process toke me sometime—I did then and even believe this more even today.)

When this all finally soaked in, I began to change my whole attitude. I was even more encouraged to change and to learn why I made the choice to act out the way I did in my past. I was not really being abandoned by God. I was not that low-life, scum of the earth. God Himself loves me so much that He took time to personally discipline me. WOW! See how this would change one's thinking, begin to change one's whole attitude, whole demeanor, to truly want to find out all of the answers to the multitude of questions that you had about your past life and why we made some of the choices that we did at those times.

This was truly a miracle, an awesome epiphany. I began to get closer to God. He is my Strength, my Comforter. God has had His Hand in my life from the "get go," then I began to realize that God really does Love me and He has plans for me, for my future; I was even more overwhelmed (in a positive way), very happy, elated. I not only had been forgiven by God, but now God has given me a purpose, a meaning, and wants to propel me into the future that He has planned or me—from my birth. (Turning our scars of the past into bright stars that enlighten the rest of our days.)

This was an awesome feeling. If God loves me, if God has forgiven me, I needed to learn to forgive myself as well.

If I cannot forgive myself on a deep and personal level, I will not be able to continue my forgiveness journey. Now at that time I didn't understand. (You'll see later.)

I began to read different books on self-forgiveness; I began to read different books on "inner child work," learning to take care of the inner child that is within all of us. This was very touching and emotional reading, and this inner child work helps us walk through a lot of our childhood issues on into our adult issues. Then, of course, I was able to read many encouraging things about forgiveness from the Bible as well. The Bible is a great book to study. God forgives us, and He teaches us to forgive others through His Word.

I wanted to change; I wanted to declare Victory in my life. I understood just how important it was to love myself, in a healthy way. When I began to like myself, I was more open and receptive to helping others. I was feeling more confident in myself. I felt good reaching out to others.

So when you begin to truly love yourself, it will show. You will begin to feel better about yourself, about your day, about your whole life. Not every day will be "Sunshine and Rainbows"; loving yourself is so empowering, so powerful—one will have HOPE getting through some of their toughest times. You know that God loves you; you are one of God's very own, very special and unique children; you are one of a kind and God loves every inch of you. (He does not like any of your inappropriate behavior. He LOVES the real you, the one He Himself has blessed into this world that we all live in today.) You have this relationship with God (your Higher Power) even through you may be fighting it right now. That's okay. God has all of the time in the world to wait on you to accept Him, but we don't have all that time.

This is like your very own children; you may not approve of all the things that your child(ren) has done or are still doing. These are your children; they are a very part of you; they are the "fruit of your loins"; how can you not still love them and want to help them all that you can? God sees us in the same way. We are the very "fruits of His Blessings"; we are the sons and daughters of the most High God (Your Higher Power). God will not like all of the choices and decisions that we make, but He still loves us.

There is not one thing that we have done in our lives or not one thing that we will do in our future that will surprise God. He knows what He was getting into when he made us. This is not to give us permission to screw up our lives and others and then expect God to clean up our mess because we know that He will forgive us. Know that God loves you and He wants you to have a great life (you have the Power to choose—life or death). He has plans for you and your future. It's His love and commitment to us (then our personal "Fee Will" commitment) is where we make the choice to do what is right and what God wants us to do.

Please trust me when I say to you all of these journeys that you will be taking in your life will probably be too difficult for you to tackle on your own.

You will need help, guidance, comforting, consoling, and nurturing along the way. May this be with a trusted friend or family member, GOD, someone that you feel God has directed you to, or even a therapist. You are a very special human being, and you deserve to live the best life that God has already planned for you. You are the only one that will have to live with yourself twenty-four seven, the rest of your life, so let's make this as enjoyable as possible, embrace yourself, and love the one that is the closest to you—YOU!

LOVE YOUR ENEMIES

Jesus said: "But I say to you, love your enemies, bless those who curse you, do good to those who spitefully use you and persecute you…" Matthew 5:44

One of the next things that I was to do was to forgive my enemies. In order to move on in my "Forgiveness Process," I needed to forgive all of those that hurt me, abused me, wronged me in my life. When I heard this, I became extremely angry; outraged would be a better suited word to all of this. How in the hell was I to forgive all of those who molested, bullied, and stolen my childhood away from me? All of those that laughed and ridiculed me, mocked, and made fun of me during my whole life. All of these things happened to me, these people aided in ruining my life; they all contributed to stealing my future away from me. There was no way I was going to forgive anyone for all of these atrocities in my life.

I was fuming. My body was shaking with anger and rage. All of these things that had happened to me were flooding my mind. All of these things happened to me, these people were wrong in what THEY did to me. I felt justified in my anger and my rage that I had for all of these people, which included my mom, dad, other family members and peers, of that time era. "How in the hell can I forgive any of these people for the devastation that they have caused me in my life? All of this… this…BS I have endured, a lot of my sick and distorted thoughts, beliefs, even some of my behavior has roots in all of the BS that has been done to me." I have tears flowing; my anger and rage is flowing. I was feeling a deep hurt inside of me. I was thinking and feeling that by forgiving all of these people, for what was done to me was saying all of those things were not all that bad, that it was okay. "Thank you, I forgive you," and go on with my life. Even worse yet, by forgiving, I believed at that time, I would be saying in essence that no damage was done, I'm cool.

I was so hurt and distraught at this thought. Needless to say I slowly began to calm down, take a minute—to breathe, so I could begin to listen to what was said to me next.

What happened to me was real, what happened to me was very wrong and should not have ever happened (in any time era.) All of the things that Mom, Dad, Grandma, other family, friends, and peers did to me was not right; just like all the bad things that I did were terribly wrong as well.

All of the things that happened to me, as a child on into my teens, these people that perpetrated on me…were wrong. That none of the mental, physical, psychological, sexual abuse should have ever happened to me or to any of you, but very sorry to say—it did happen. It happened maybe years ago.

Now let's look at how I reacted to having someone just suggesting for me to forgive the people that harmed me, as a child in particular. I was filled with anger, rage, resentment, my blood pressure was extremely high, and if I would have had a weak heart, I would have been in the hospital, if not worse…. All of those years of holding all of this back, all of those years of stuffing all of this anger, rage, hatred, very deep-seeded resentment, some will erupt. Try to imagine the stress on your nerves, your heart, your blood pressure, and God only knows all of the other things that this rage was doing to us. This is not to hurt you, but out of pure respect for you:

"Where has all of that anger, rage, and resentment gotten you?" All of these things have happened to you—years ago. The ones that abused you, most of them do not care for you or want anything to do with you. Now let's stop giving them this power over you today. "No one has power over me!" one might blurt out.

True, still, every time that you keep remembering all of those things that have happened to you; every time you hold onto all of that anger and rage for what was done—-you are allowing them to control you by all of the emotions that you still have for them. Now is the time to begin to let all of that go; all of these things did happen—maybe a long time ago. You are allowing yourself to relive this torment all the time.

This whole forgiveness journey is for our mental health. This journey is so very important to us all.

When we are asked to forgive our predators, we are not being asked to forget all that they have done to us; what they did to us was wrong, it happened, it was reality, and it hurt us badly, deeply. By forgiving them, WE are beginning to let go of that pain that we have been holding on to for so long. The predator(s) is not physically hurting us anymore, but WE are repeating all of this pain, in our mind. We are letting all of that pain, that "power" to control us. We have thoughts about this, our thoughts; we let them affect our feelings and, if we allow them, can and will control our behavior. So when we forgive someone, we are not letting them "off the hook" for anything. We are realizing that we cannot change the past. What has happened is done and over with now. "Water under a far and distant bridge, that happened many years ago."

Now we are adults; we have the power and control over our future and carrying all that ole' baggage, all of these resentments around from years, is not good for us. It's been destroying our health, for some time, really. So let's really begin to let all of that garbage that we have been carrying around for all of those years—choose to let it go!

This part of our journey will be difficult. I mean we have been carrying all of this pain and agony around for so long. Every problem that we have ever had we have blamed it on that person, those people, places, or things. "If only this didn't happen to me, then I would not be going through all of this hell and torment today." We will have to stop this blame game too. I'm seeing "Atlas" (from Greek Mythology) with the weight of the world on his shoulders. That's us. It doesn't have to be us. We can make that decision today to begin this forgiveness process right now.

It will take some very serious hard work, but we can do it, how do I know this, I don't even know you? First, if I can walk through this "Forgiveness Journey", anyone can walk this journey. Second, God would never ask us to do anything that He has not already given us power to do.

All through the Bible God has told us to forgive our enemies, to pray for our enemies, and not to curse them. (Romans 12:19–21) **Begin to think**, God has forgiven us for all of our sins; now who are we not to forgive the ones that have done us wrong. When someone has done you wrong, give all of this to the Lord. "Revenge is mine! says the Lord!!" God will take care of things—in His time and not ours. Then holding onto all of the anger and rage about who has done you wrong is not helping you at all. Let it go; forgive them and go on your way—life is way too short for all of this unwanted stress, pain, and agony to weigh down your life any longer.

So how does one begin their "Forgiveness Journey?"

> Start with making a list of the people that you feel have harmed you, whom you NEED to forgive. (If I would say make a list of people that you want to forgive there probably would be a couple of names on your list, if any at all.)

> After making your list, then begin with the person that you feel has hurt you the worst. A lot of the ole thoughts and feelings will begin to come up again when you think of these people.

All of those hateful thoughts you have for these people, all of that anger and rage that you are still feeling for them will come rushing back on you. You are also feeling all of the body sensations that you are still having every time that you think of them. All of those things you are still letting effect you, that is power that you are still giving that person to have over you. Every second that you think of those people, every ounce of fear that you still may have is all a form of power that you give them to control you just one more time. (You may not have seen or been around them for years. They may have passed away years ago.)All of that power belongs to you; take all of that power back; proclaim "Victory!" in your life and—just forgive them. This is for your sake, for your mental health, for your health. Each person that you forgive, then, you will need to give that person to God (Your Higher Power); proclaim to God that you have forgiven this person for all of the devastation that they have caused in your life. You forgive them, and now you give this person to God to let Him decide on what to do with them. Then it is not your problem to worry about any longer; if God chooses to do nothing than that is God's decision. Let Him handle things. When you put this kind of trust in the Lord (Your Higher Power) you can enjoy your forgiveness journey even more.

> Take your time working with each person on your list. You may have to go over and over a particular person on the list; this is okay too. All of this is to help you, to help you take back all of this power that you have given so many people in your life—for so long. Some of us are still holding on to all of this anger and rage from our childhoods, of things people have done to us; some of these people are not even alive, others are not even living around us any longer. All of those people do not care about us; they are living their lives and could not care less about us. Then here we are, wanting to let these people control us to this day. I say enough is enough, and we are taking back our power this day—TODAY!
Another thing that I done was, as I was working through my list, I would also try to see why that person(s) had done what they did to me. Not to get

myself all angry and enraged again; not to justify what they done to me, just trying to understand why. First and foremost is, as the "victim," we did not do anything wrong. What happened to us was not our fault; we were innocent in all of these situations; we are trying to understand why that person chose to do what they did to us.

For instance, my mom: I have shared how overprotective, smothering, and very dominate and controlling that she was of me. How I could not go and play with the kids in the neighborhood. It was a feat to let me join the Cub Scouts; she wanted me near her at all times. All of the anger and rage that I had for her and all of her years of dominance on my life.

> I asked myself WHY? I call this my "Onion Clock Process": peeling back the layers of the problem to see why it ticks.

After really putting some thought into this, a lot of my thoughts and feelings began to change for my mother. See, Mom had lost one child before me, and she had a few problems having me even. I remember Mom and Grandma telling me of different times that Mom and Dad thought they almost lost me as a baby, due to a number of different sicknesses. So a lot of Mom's over-protectiveness was due to her love for me: she didn't want me to get sick, she didn't want me to get hurt, and she loved me so much that she didn't want to lose me. So, she chose to smother me, the only way she knew how to keep me safe and alive. (Which really didn't help me either in the long run.)

Then I began to look at some of the other issues that I had with Mom, and I was understanding more and more now why she may have done some of the things she did to me. The verbal sexual abuse was wrong unequivocally! This happened when I was eight years old; the other mental and physical abuses were defiantly wrong too.

When I was in therapy, I was thirty-eight or thirty-nine years old. I needed to forgive Mom for this and let it go. (It had been over thirty years ago at that time.) It's done. That happened many moons ago. There is nothing that can be changed or made better in my past. I'm, finally tired of carrying all of this garbage with me. I will not allow her to steal one more day of my life. God rest her soul, my mother passed a few years ago; it's been time to take back all of that power that I was still allowing her to steal from me. Like the ole' TV cartoon, "I Have The Power!"—really, I always did, then I just began to see it—soon, I began to feel it.

> > Once we have gone through your forgiveness journey, there will still be times when we will begin to blame this or blame that on our past. We need to stop ourselves right then and there. We will need to remind ourselves that we have forgiven that person, take that responsibility ourselves, and feel good about the power that we now have to change and manage our lives.

Like I have said, this "Forgiveness Journey" will take a lot of hard work; our life evolved over years, so this forgiveness journey will take some time too, but we all can do it. This will be awesome. Do what you can as often as you can, reap your rewards as you travel down your "Forgiveness Journey." Keep your eyes on that small, faint flicker of light in the far distance—that is HOPE; you will need every ounce of it traveling this journey.

This journey has worked for me and for many others too. You need to want to change your life; you need to want to take back that power and control that was stolen from you years ago. Then channel all of that into your future, with God (or your Higher Power) by your side, helping you through your "Forgiveness Process," this will be an awesome journey for you. It has been for many that have taken this journey before and all that will after you.

The oxymoron of all of this is "predator forgiveness" will empower you, your life, and your whole future.

The paradox is when you go through this "Forgiveness Journey"; you forgive those who have hurt you, you will begin to feel this empowering feeling in your life. This freedom is a very empowering, awesome paradox—that will take time for some—remember that this is okay too.

Remember this: you had no control over what happened in your past, as a child—as an adult, you can't change a thing either. You do have full and complete control over how you will live the rest of your life—choose a happy, joyful and FULL LIFE… Let that veil of darkness you have chosen to carry with you all of these years—

"LET IT ALL GO!"

Begin to bask in the light you are now letting into your life. Enjoy and rejoice in this empowerment—you deserve it.

Part II: The Butterfly

Stage V
You Are A Survivor

"Today Is The First Day Of The Rest Of Your Life…!!" This is the day which the LORD has made; we will rejoice and be glad in it. Psalm 118:24

This is nothing new to us, really—we have always been survivors. We have all went through some type of trials and tribulations our whole lives of one degree or another. We are all fighters; some of us are still trying to nurse these scars, these deep wounds from our past—with little to no hope for a peaceful, fulfilling life.

Anything in life that is worth much will only be achieved through hard work, blood, sweat, and tears, sacrifice, even with pain, suffering, and a lot of God's Love, Forgiveness, Compassion, and Direction. God (or your Higher Power) will never ask you to do anything that you are not capable of doing already. You have the very "seeds of change" within you. God knows because He has put them there, personally, before you were ever born. *Now it is up to you to want to water them*; you must be willing to do the work, to water these seeds, to nurture the seeds, to weed all of the old thoughts and old feelings of doubt. When they come to try to smother the life out of your changes that you are making and the new dreams you are beginning to envision will begin to blossom.

"All the Flowers of tomorrow are in the seeds of Today!" (Proverbs)

Begin to feed and nurture the butterflies of your life; stop feeding any of the monsters.

The definition of insanity is doing the very same thing over and over again hoping for different results. We have carried all of this hurt, pain, agony, anger, resentment, and rage about people and/or things that have happened to us in our past for way, way too long. In all do respect, where has all of the rage and resentment gotten us?

All of this has gotten us nowhere, but we are still putting ourselves through all of this heartache, pain, and misery. There is not one thing that can be done, changed, or made different about the past; this is why it is so vital for us to stop giving all of these people, places, and/or things power over our lives any longer.

Truth be known, if one was able to make right all of the wrongs that have been done to them (I mean like punishing, beating, hurting their predators—badly, even suing them financially)—if, and I do mean—*if*—there was any degree of satisfaction or relief, it would only be temporary, because we refuse to let all of those things go; our thoughts will still be so vivid, and that pain will still feel so real. (One maybe sitting on mounds of cash; what about the horrid thoughts and nightmares that one may still allow to plague their lives.) Even if you took it upon yourself to dish out revenge upon any of the people that have harmed you—the taste of revenge would be like a "Drug," that high (if you would even have one) will soon wear off, and you will soon go back to your ole "crap pile" that you are still so accustomed to going to—once again.

Unless, unless, we truly begin our "Forgiveness Journey." This is so vital to your Survivor Process because it is during that process that we begin to let go of all the ole baggage that "we" have chosen to drag with us all of these years.

Once again, please do not ever think that I am trying to lessen or question any of the horrors that you have gone through as a child or in your past, because I'm not in any way doing that or suggesting that at all. The whole forgiveness process ***is for you, for your mental health,*** for ***your future peace of mind and wellbeing***. It is okay to let all of those things go.

You now know that there is nothing you can do about any of the past, so let it go. All of the people that have hurt you, in your past, are either dead, dying, or have totally moved on with their lives and could not care about you at all. (I'm truly sorry—reality bites sometimes.) It's time for you to do the same—move on! "It's not right what they have done to me and to others!" you rightfully point out. Yes, justice needs to be done, but that is not our job; give it ALL to your Higher Power…Work with the authorities and others for some solace.

"Revenge is mine," says the Lord, let the Lord take care of these things in

"His Way" and in "His Time." He can do something about these things where we can't. Whatever we would do would not take our suffering away from us.

We need to focus on to change the things that we do have the power and control over…

This would be US; we have the power over our thoughts, which feed into how we feel. (By wanting to control/change our thoughts we will control and can change our feelings.) Then you will see how by controlling your thoughts and feelings, you have total control over your behaviors, which will soon begin to change as well. For instance, I felt so hurt, neglected, and disowned by my father as a child. It seemed like he was always drunk or always drinking. My mom and dad seemed to always be arguing fussing and verbally fighting about something. Then hearing my mom and grandma keep saying how worthless and no good my dad was (how no good men were as a whole), how he was a drunken, good-for-nothing man, I began to think and feel that same way. I thought that Dad was so hung up on his drinking and hanging out with his buddies and he had no time for me. I had so much hate, anger, and resentment for him as a child, I felt like I was the only kid alive without a father back then. I hated him for that.

It was not until I was in therapy that I began to look at the other side— remember, that there are always two sides to every story. (This is not to let my dad off the hook for anything that he has done to me or the family. It's beginning to try to understand "Why?" he was doing some of these things.)(Learning Victim Empathy.)

Here I was, beginning to see that there was a lot going on in my Dad's life as well.

> He had completed two to three different tours in the navy during WWII, and how traumatic that this had to be on him and all the men at that time. How tragic, absolutely overwhelming, things had to have been during those times. I could not begin to imagine. Then coming back to the States after all of the hell that one has been in for so long and try to live a normal life again…? Not having the doctors or the mental health programs to help them through their post-traumatic stress did not help at all. Those horrors of war must be mind blowing.

> Then soon getting married, then the responsibility of a family, trying to balance a job, family, and keep peace in the family, I guess must have been too much, and he felt that his only recourse was the booze and his friends.

Of course, as a child, I never thought of things that way. I heard and felt it was all Dad's fault because of his drinking is why we were going through all the things that we were at that time. So, the more I began to think about Dad and some of the things that he had went through and was going through, I was beginning to see Dad in a different light. Things were not *all* Dad's fault; things were not all of Mom's fault. I soon began to look at the other people, places, and things in my life with a new, fresh perspective. Guess what? Over time, that was, over time, my anger, rage, and resentment became less and less. I soon gave all of that up as I was trying to understand the "Why?" (my "Onion Clock Process") behind different things. Again, this does not excuse my father from the things that he did. I was trying to understand more of "Why?" and this helped me through a lot.

One of the other things that I wanted to hear from my father as a child was three words: "I love you." He has told my sisters that many a time, but not once did I hear the words from him personally to me. I let that bother me very deeply. Again, during therapy is when I began to really look at some of the reasons why.

> Some of our parents emulate how they were raised; considering the era in time my father was raised, his father probably did not tell his sons that he loved them, either. It may not have been the right thing to do, for a father to tell his son(s) that he loved him, back then, in their childhood days.

My dad *showed* his love for me, by always having a roof over our head, food in our stomachs, clothes on our back, and schooling was always paid. He was always there when I was sick to help out when and where he could during those times. As a child, I would like to have heard the words; they are so precious and profound to me—I didn't. Therapy helped me to see that even though my father did not say the words "I love you," the proof was all around me. Oh, how this helped in my forgiveness with my father.

I was so blessed. I saw my father the last few hours that he was with us, before he went to be with the Lord; I patted his hand, looked into his eyes, and said, "I Love You, Dad." With a smile on his face, he looked up at me and said, "Me too," which to me that meant that he loved me too. I cried every time that I cherished that moment. (I'm still emotional re-thinking of it to this day.) If I had not went through my forgiveness process concerning my father, I would have missed those last precious words that I heard my father say; words that I had waited my lifetime to hear. There was proof all around me, I just didn't want to see it.

"Forgiveness" is the key to empowering the rest of your life, a beautiful paradox; I cannot stress this enough.

I spent my whole childhood and young adult life with all of this anger, rage, and resentment toward my family, people, and places around me—for what? Did all of this make me feel better? NO. Did any of this empower me or protect me during all of that time? I may have thought so at the time; again, the answer is NO. Yet I embraced all of these resentments as a "shield of protection." I was not going to let anyone get that close to me again to hurt me. But I still felt hurt and alone all of my life. All of that energy that I wasted on hating my family, friends, places, and things, was energy that I chose to waste myself. Until I was in therapy and the day that they talked about "Forgiveness" and how enraged I got to even think of forgiving the people that I thought that hurt me, was totally and completely absurd at that moment. It was explained to me that "Forgiveness" does not mean what happened to us didn't happen or this forgiveness doesn't let those people off the hook, nor say what happened to us was not tragic. "Forgiveness" is not like that at all; this is a process that we need to do for *"Us,"* for *our wellbeing* and *mental health* and for no one else. What happened to us should not have happened; we didn't do a thing to cause/deserve the problems— these things did happened. There was nothing that we could have done back then, just like we can't change the things that did happen to us back then at this time. In all do respect, I must then ask you the very question that I was asked back then (once again): "Where has all of that anger, rage, and resentment got you?" "What do I have from carrying all of that burden, all of that hell and torment with me for all of those years?" A resounding…Nothing! Just more heartache, pain, more anger, rage and resentment (a lot more gray hair) that I have let continue to steal my joy, happiness, and my power out of my life. I am here to tell you that this "Forgiveness" was and is the key to empowering and taking control of your life once again. (A control that we have had all along…)

"Vengeance is MINE, says the Lord!" Let God (or your Higher Power) have all that pain, and He will deal with things as He sees fit, in His time.

You will soon feel this freedom; over time, it will feel like the weight of your world is being lifted from your shoulders—live—now live the best life that your Higher Power wants for you to live—chose LIFE!

I know and fully understand how extremely hard and very difficult all of this was for me. For all of us that have been raised in a "War Zone" so to speak—our whole childhoods, most of our adult lives—this "Forgiveness Journey" will seem almost impossible for you to even begin. You need to see that very small flicker of light at that far distance of all your darkness that you may be seeing at this time. That little flicker of light is called *"Hope"*; we all have and can see that flicker of light in the far, far distance. For some of us, it just seems further away, maybe even harder to see. It's vitally important for all of us to never lose sight of that flicker of light no matter how small it may seem at the present time. That light has been calling to you for years; all you have to do is begin your journey. You must make the decision to reach for it and to one day grasp it, embrace it, to begin to experience the peace and joy in your life that has always been there; you just have not felt worthy to accept it...

That "Light," that "Hope" is all yours; no one can take this away from us. We must work hard to make the changes needed in our lives, so we can one day bask in this immense light for the rest of our days.

You Are a Butterfly

Begin to see yourself as a Butterfly.

First Stage: The Egg to Baby: This is you being formed inside your mother's womb. This is your very special beginning. You are very unique; you are a very, very special life form. There will only be one of you to bless this world. (I know you may not feel like it right now, but you are; hopefully, you will be able to see how awesome you are soon.)

Second Stage: Infancy to Teen: Here is where your parent(s) will care for you, love you, and nurture you into your teens. They will feed, care for you; here is where you will grow very quickly. Here is where a lot of morals, beliefs, and knowledge will begin to form you. This is a special unique stage for you in your development. A lot of good and bad things may happen to you and how you begin to see life in general. (Good traits and bad traits will begin to form as well.)

Third Stage: Teenage Years: At this stage you will continue to grow, learn from your environment (Good or Bad). A lot your personal traits will continue to be learned, and you will begin to form the special—you. Learning and forming your own thoughts, feelings, and behaviors. This will be very vital to your development.

Fourth Stage: Adult/Butterfly: You are very beautiful and free. Here you can decide on what you want to be the rest of your life. You have total and complete control over who you are and who you want to become.(Good or Bad.) You can choose to be a beautiful butterfly and/or an ugly moth. At this time, you will decide. Will you let the negative experiences of your life define you, or will you choose to grow into the awesome butterfly that you were born to be at your very beginning?

Every one of us has had rough things, bad times, that we had to work through in our lives. Some of us have literally been through hell and back, to say the least. Will we let all of this define who we are the rest of our lives, or will we turn all those lemons, that life deals to us, into the best lemonade that we can?

We can choose to turn all of our scares into stars.

Scars Into Stars

All Things Happen For A Reason; All Things Work Out For the Betterment of Good and For The Glory Of God! Romans 8:28

These words were not meant to make light of the past that we went through at all; this is another way to try to understand what did happen. It was not your fault because of what happened to you as young children. It was not God's Fault (nor your Higher Power's fault) for all of the things that have happened to you. I am not here to defend God (or your Higher Power) for interceding or not interceding on your behalf (this will be something to ask Him—when you see Him once again). What I am here to tell you is that GOD loves you. He always has loved you, and all of those things God is wanting to heal. God is wanting to turn all of your hurt, pain, devastation, anger, rage, and resentments, ALL of your scars, He will turn into stars—if you let Him—if you will allow Him to. All of those things that I went through as a child just didn't happen for no reason. I know that doesn't make much sense right now; it didn't to me when I first tried to wrap my head around that thought process back then.

I am here to tell you that everything that I went through growing up (some I have shared here with you all) was to be able to help the soon millions that have gone through what I have or a lot worse—to show them that there is HOPE.

Hope is another one of those seeds that I have been talking about throughout this book. One must have HOPE; having hope opens the door to looking at other things like change, love, soon forgiveness, and continuing on into your "Survivor Process." I'm not for a minute making light of any of the things that has happened to you (or to me), but I understand that if these things didn't happen (to me), I would not be able to share all of what I have with you today. I would not be able to give you hope that no matter what has happened to you, you have the power to take full control over your life—now. To live a better life, the best life that one can live if you so choose to. Yes, these are scares that will be with us forever, but here we are today; we have been through Hell's fire and damnation. We are "Survivors!" Let's share what we have learned to get us here today with others that have or are going through much worse than we ever did—share our now "Stars" of hope and love. It is very important for you to see that God (your Higher Power) loves you: He always has loved you, He will never ever abandon you. (You are children of the Most High God) To come back to God, ask Him how He wants to complete your life, ask Him how He is going to turn your "Scars Into Stars."

It's time you take back this power in your life. God Bless you and all of your loved ones!

In closing,

Three things will last forever—faith, hope, and love—and the greatest of these is LOVE. 1 Corinthians 13:13

Out of total respect to you and to all victims, I write this book to give you all HOPE. To help you to see that you do not have to live in your pain any longer. That you and only you have the power to change, and your "Higher Power" will be right beside you all the way through your life's journey.

There are hundreds, thousands, maybe even millions of good and honest people in this world that we live in today. (It may be hard to believe, but this is true.) (Even in total contradiction of today's ongoing events.) "TRUST—But Verify"

Your children are the most precious beings that God has given to you, to care for and to nurture. Please make sure that they know that you LOVE them and care for them very much. Today, with way to many single-parent families, or where both parents must have full-time jobs, I understand how hard this maybe.

Once again, out of total respect only and not to scare anyone: "If you do not take time to show your child(ren) that you LOVE them, *someone else will be more than happy to.*" Please let your children know that they can share anything with you at any time. They need to be able to "trust" their parents above anyone and everyone else in their lives. This is so vital and extremely important—*NEVER* be too busy to spend "*quality* time" with your children—with your family. Know your children, know their mood swings, some of their habits—learn, know, and share in their happiness; be very observant and passionate when it seems that they may be going through some tough times. Be the kind and loving parent (that you may have wished for); let them see and know that you are there for them at all times—NO matter what they may be going through. Some of the things your children may be going through may seem so small and trivial to you but are important to your child. Be compassionate; do your best to see the issues through their eyes; and share some of your wisdom to help them through these troubling times. They will love you for it. You may say: "None of this was done for me when I was growing up. Mom had to have two full-time jobs and us kids turned out okay!"

"Awesome—great, all of us choose to handle issues differently; it would always be nice to have a kind, compassionate, and wise person to guide us through the trouble waters of that time, your children especially." Be very vigilante and notice when your normal extrovert of a child becomes quiet, meek, and withdrawn. Also stay vigilante when your introvert child becomes even more withdrawn or more meek than usual—worst yet, more angry and aggressive. No need to panic; it may mean nothing. Take time with the child to see what maybe be going on with them. Do not approach them angry and condescending. They love you, they may need your assistance navigating these troubled times. Now would be a good time to show the child just how important they are to you, how much that they mean to you; listen to what is bothering them. Truly listen to what they are saying, no matter how difficult it maybe. Do your best not to overreact and scare them by whatever they may be sharing with you. Listen closely to them; be sure that you understand what has happened; be sure to get as many details and facts that they are willing to share with you at that time. This is a very extremely, very important "bonding moment" for them and you. Do not take this time lightly.

Whatever the issue is, do not make light of things, do not laugh, make fun of them or seem to be condescending in any way. They may be going through something that is so trivial to you, or it's natural for their age, something that you will be able to personally help and guide the child through. If not, seek the necessary help that is needed to get your child and yourself through this issue. Embrace them, showing the child that you do understand and are willing to help them through this issue or any issue. So they will know that whatever happens, you are and will always be there to help them.

Heaven forbid, when or if something would ever happen, you will be there for them—ALWAYS! I know that what I'm about to say will be extremely difficult to do:

<Do your very best to stay calm. This is your child, who is sharing what has or is happening to them; they are scared, confused, maybe hurting mentally, maybe even physically. You must be there—calmly as can be.

> Asking and closely listening to everything they a sharing with you, closely listening to all the facts of what happened—no matter how difficult it will be to listen too.

> NEVER, I mean never let your child believe that you do not believe or trust what they are sharing with you. It's imperative for you to fully listen to them *"Trust and Verify"* all that they have shared with you.

Then act accordingly to the true facts, no matter your findings. PLEASE act quickly, as calmly as possible (not frantically or aggressively). You are there to help your child through this ordeal, not to load more toxic shame and toxic guilt upon them. (They will do that to themselves.) Whatever this issue may be (mental, physical or sexual abuse), the child may already think they are to blame—they've done something wrong to cause all of this to happen to them. The child needs your love, support, and ongoing reassurance (that they are innocent, that they did nothing wrong), that you will handle this problem quickly and effectively—wisely.

> Reporting your findings to the proper authorities.

> If warranted, take your child to the hospital to be evaluated.

> ALL hospitals are "Court-Mandated Reporters"; they must notify the proper authorities of this issue.

> Some hospitals have or are connected to a "Crisis Team" that can and

will help your child and you through this crisis. Some can and will take an account of what happened to save your child of repeatedly going though this horrific event(s) over and over again.

> Your child needs you by their side, loving, caring for them through all of this. You must be their "Rock."

Please, do not try to take matters into your own hands; you have alerted the authorities, let them do their job. Your child and you need to stay safe.

> Your only job will be helping your child throughout this ordeal.
> Follow up with the authorities, be an asset to helping the authorities ALL you can. Be as assertive as need to be, not overly aggressive.
> Do your best to protect your child, your children all you can throughout this ordeal.
> Also you must take care of yourself; how can you ever care for your child if you don't take care of yourself...?

STOP! Blaming yourself for any of what has happened to your child.
THIS IS NOT YOUR FAULT EITHER.

You are and have been doing all you can. Stop beating yourself up. You know now some of what happened, and you are in full control of things, taking care of your child and their needs as they arise. You are keeping your child as safe as you can; this is your precious baby, they need you more coherent now than ever.

> Take time to pray, pray to your Higher Power to help you and your family through all of this. Don't blame your Higher Power; this is not their fault either.
> If follow-up therapy is suggested, personally choose a child therapist you can trust. If you or any of your family members need help, don't hesitate to seek help for them and/or with them.
> "Stay cool, calm, and collective" as a parent can possibly be through all of this. All of your empathy needs to be for your child and your family.

I apologize for any hurt that I may cause to what I'm about to say next; giving a legitimate guilt trip, only if needed. As they say, "If the shoe fits wear it." If this guilt trip is warranted, you need to correct things ASAP.

> IF you think or you know that something BAD is happening to your precious child and you have not or refuse to do anything to save your child from this hellish nightmare, you are an "accessory" to the perpetrator, and something needs to change immediately! If your child has even come to you telling you of these heinous things are happening to them, you refuse to believe them or to help them in any way, you are as guilty of the crimes against your child as the predator. It's a terrible, horrific ordeal to be abused by anyone at any time in their life. Then for them to know that someone knows about all of this, and that person(s) is not helping to save them, (for whatever that person's justification may be). The victim also will feel as deeply betrayed with these people as they do with the predator.

> I plead with you—stop whatever passive BS you are justifying telling yourself and aid the child—NOW! Before it is too late to do anything for your child.

> Not all kind adults are pedophiles or rapists. Most of the adults that are helping your children are very kind, and they love helping children in a healthy, positive way. Be observant, stay aware of how your child is acting, how their behaviors may be changing. "When you have doubt—don't shout" or scream; lovingly check with your child to see what maybe going on with them. Most of the time it will be nothing. You will not know until you ask.

> Pedophiles can be older males or older females. Don't ever believe that your child cannot be abused by the opposite sex. I have been in heart wrenching groups where the predator was being abused by an older female as a child, and nothing was done. This person, and many others like him, chose to be a bad person when they grew older. Yes, this was their choice.

> NOT all pedophiles or rapists are registered, nor on a state or federal watch list/registries. Check and verify as you see fit—watch your child's behavior will be your best checklist for you to follow. If this may help any, three percent or less of registered pedophiles/sex offenders (this is nationwide now) ever reoffend, ever hurt another child or adult. Above all else, stay a caring and loving parent, and don't smother your child's childhood from them. "TRUST—and VERIFY" when you have doubts.

FOOD FOR THOUGHT:

All people on the face of this earth have been placed here with a purpose, with true meaning, and every one of us has a God -Given Destiny. All six-plus billion of us are all parts of one body; each and everyone one of us has a positive meaning and an awesome purpose.

The <u>"Purpose"</u>: To love your Higher Power with all of your heart, mind and soul.
> Then to love yourself and one another as He Loves you. That is all of our purpose in life.

Our "God-Given Destinies," our meaning, will be between your Higher Power and you. This is where you will need to search for Him, pray to Him, and in His time He will reveal to you what you are to do (if anything is different than what you are doing right now, listen, and heed to your Higher Power's Request). As you begin to search Him, soon getting to know Him, He will let you know what is next in your life.

Some have waited for days, months, and even years for this to happen, so have faith the "He Who Started A Good Work In You Will Finish It," in His time now.

God started a "Good Work" in you even before the very day this world was blessed with you. God has never given up on you for a second. He loves you today just as much as the day you were born. You may not see or feel anything right now, that's okay too; all of these changes in our thinking, feeling, and behavior will happen over time. Our lives were not scarred up in a day, and it will take time for these scars to heal, and you will begin to see them as the "Stars" that they really are to you today... Over time you will learn that you can trust and love others once again. Not all people are like the predator(s) that devastated your life. You do not need to let your past control your life any longer; begin your "Survivor Journey" TODAY! "Forgive those who have hurt you as you want your Higher Power to forgive you." Remarkable things can happen in your life if you let them, and "Forgiveness" is the key to becoming a *Survivor.*

"YOU ARE A SURVIVOR—YOU HAVE THE POWER TO CHANGE THE REST OF YOUR LIFE..."
"CHOOSE LIFE AND LIVE!"
"Tough Times Don't Last—Tough People Do!"

"May God Bless You and Yours!"

One very last thing:

To the Judicial System (A word from the wise), "Hand Slaps" (probation) and a fine(for most) do not work. After the probation and the fear factor wear off, one would be right back reoffending, destroying lives once again.

Suggestion: (For Sex offenders)
> If not a prison sentence, mandate mandatory *sex offender therapy* for at least five-plus years to life.
> Or a Civil Commitment, to a sex offender program, in a prison setting, where they must show evidence of change before they are released. Just a suggestion. Just sayin'.

"Scars show us where we have been, does not have to determine where we are going!"

"Turn your face to the Sun and the shadows will fall behind you." –Maori Proverb

Take your newfound light and help others to see through their darkness...

"May God Bless you and guide you on the journey he has chosen for you... Bless you."
John Fisher